DAY CARE AND PUBLIC POLICY IN ONTARIO

Michael Krashinsky

Day Care and Public Policy in Ontario

PUBLISHED FOR THE ONTARIO ECONOMIC COUNCIL BY
UNIVERSITY OF TORONTO PRESS
TORONTO AND BUFFALO

Canadian Cataloguing in Publication Data

Krashinsky, Michael, 1947-
  Day care and public policy in Ontario

  (Ontario Economic Council research studies; 11
  ISSN 0078-5091)

  Bibliography: p.
  ISBN 0-8020-3349-0 pa.

  1. Day care centers – Ontario. 2. Day care centers –
  Ontario – Finance. I. Title. II. Series: Ontario
  Economic Council. Ontario Economic Council research
  studies; 11.

  HV861.C22055   362.7'1   C77-001405-4

This study reflects the views of the author and not necessarily those of
the Ontario Economic Council

This book has been published during the
Sesquicentennial year of the University of Toronto

For Katharine

Contents

Preface

I would like to thank the Ontario Economic Council for its help while this report was researched and written. Their generous financial assistance and moral support made possible the collecting and processing of much data and made the writing process much smoother.

Eileen McIntyre has been a dedicated and inspiring research assistant. Her extensive knowledge of the field made her invaluable in gaining access to information, and her commitment to this project made her very useful in discussing the ideas presented here.

Many others have been instrumental in the writing of this report. I wish to express my gratitude to the anonymous referees who commented upon the first draft, and to John Buttrick and Constantine Kapsalis, whose comments on a later draft were most helpful. Eileen McIntyre and Michael Sinclair made useful and extensive comments on my work. I acknowledge also the help of many others in the day care field who were extremely generous with their time. At the Metro Toronto level, Wilf Boyce and Marguerite Butt made their time available and arranged for the collection of data most useful to my work. At the provincial level, Jean Stevenson arranged access to significant amounts of information about day care in Ontario. At the federal level, George Cook and David Gower provided many data from the 1973 day care survey, and Howard Clifford was always willing to share his knowledge and ideas. This is by no means an inclusive list. The day care field includes many deeply committed people, and from the federal level down to the individual day care centres, they all were open to my inquiries.

Deborah Campbell did a careful job in typing the various drafts of this report.

Naturally, I bear full responsibility for any errors or omissions in this report.

Finally, my deepest appreciation goes to my wife Katharine. Her careful proofreading has been indispensable. She has suffered with me through writing and rewriting, and her patience and common sense have supported my work during the past year and a half.

MK

DAY CARE AND PUBLIC POLICY IN ONTARIO

1
Introduction – Day care as public policy

Day care has emerged in recent years as an issue for public policy. The debate over day care has been complicated by the widely different interests that might be served by public involvement in day care. Parents contemplating work in the labour force would view subsidized day care as a welcome benefit. Taxpayers might see day care as a way to reduce the welfare rolls and move women into the labour force. Women's rights advocates might see day care as a right of women, necessary if women are to realize themselves as individuals. Those concerned about poor children might feel that quality day care would help those children enter school on an equal footing with their more affluent peers. Day care professionals, concerned about low quality day care, might suggest regulations to restrict the kind of day care available in the marketplace.

The debate over day care has come to a head at this time because of the recent rapid entry into the labour force of mothers with young children. So long as most children were cared for in their own homes by their families, the state generally remained out of the area. With rare exceptions of extreme abuse, it was generally agreed that parents alone could be responsible for judging and serving the needs of their children. But when more and more children are cared for out of the home, and when cash changes hands in the marketplace for this care, it becomes much easier for the state to take an interest. The public concern for the welfare of children, especially when these children are not cared for by their parents, practically ensures that the state will take that interest.

The debate over day care is not, however, a technical one over the merits of alternative forms of child care. Day care subsidies will involve real redistributions of income in society, and those subsidies represent a very real increase in the public's financial share of the costs of child raising – and as any parent knows, those costs are high (not only in terms of money spent, but in terms of income forgone when a parent leaves the labour force and stays at home to raise children).[1]

Economic analysis cannot resolve a question that is fundamentally political. What the economist can do, and what this report attempts to do, is to ask whether a certain set of policies are the best way to achieve a given set of goals. In general, this report will argue that the day care subsidies are a poor way to redistribute income, and that current policies have tended to be inefficient – that is, that other policies would achieve the desired goals at far less cost to society. The report does not argue against redistributing income, only against doing so inefficiently.

It is clear that many of the arguments for day care focus on subsidies as an efficient way to benefit both taxpayers and poor families. The following quote should illustrate this view:

Julia Schultz also pointed out the high cost to the taxpayer, resulting, in the long run, from the absence of day care. One obvious example, she said, was that of mothers being forced onto the welfare rolls because of present inadequate and often expensive day care (*Day Care for Everyone,* November 1972, p. 2).

This report will argue that reductions in the high tax rate on women's earnings (especially the earnings of women on welfare) will be far more efficient than subsidies to day care and will achieve the same goals.

Because the care of children is an emotional issue, day care represents fertile ground on which to fight for change. And day care is a new sector. Changes in policy can be achieved without a large body of laws and expectations to make change both difficult and expensive. But as will become clear, large comprehensive day care programs will be expensive, and rational policy making would make much more sense financially.

1 Much of the rhetoric reveals the commitment by many day care advocates to a redistribution of income and responsibility. For example, in an OFL submission to the Ontario Government: 'Child care, which is of prime importance to the majority of Ontario parents, must no longer be considered a welfare measure but rather a right for every child.' And later in the same submission: 'The cost of quality care will remain prohibitive until the government enacts legislation providing for corporate financing of child care services. Those who benefit the most should carry the cost. The funds so acquired should be used to develop universal child care available as a right to all parents and children' (Ontario Federation of Labour, CLC, Submission to the Government of Ontario, *Legislative Proposals 1975,* p. 20).

The reader should note that in this study, when day care policy is discussed, the term day care will usually refer to care given in a day care centre to the children of working mothers. In the past, a significant portion of the subsidized day care places in Ontario have gone to children whose parents are unable to care for them for reasons other than labour force participation (for example, in cases of mental illness, alcoholism, physical disability, etc.). By and large, this type of care has filled a real need, and in no way is it suggested that it be terminated. The focus here is on day care for working mothers simply because this is now the major area of debate on day care.

Day care has also been considered in the law in Ontario to include part-time institutions, like nursery schools, whose main function has been part-time care for children whose mothers do not work. Although some discussion is given to subsidies to nursery schools in Chapter 5, the prime concern of this report is child care to fill the needs of working mothers.

This report may be divided into three main sections. Chapters 2 and 3 attempt to set the stage for the reader, laying out as clearly as possible the present child care situation in Ontario and its historical development. Chapter 2 concentrates on the growing entry of mothers into the labour force and examines the arrangements being made for the care of their children. The growing public subsidy to day care is documented. Chapter 3 examines the cost of child care both in and out of day care centres. Some proposals for reducing costs are examined and the possible sacrifice in quality in any reduction is considered.

Chapters 4 and 5 discuss the whole area of subsidies to day care. Chapter 4 concentrates on a more theoretical investigation of the rationales for day care subsidies and the efficiency of a subsidy program. Chapter 5 applies this theory to evaluate the current day care program, and proposals are made for improvement.

Chapter 6 looks at the issue of regulation. The nature of day care as an economic commodity is discussed and different ways of providing day care – public, commercial, co-operative, and non-profit – are examined. Suggestions for the future are advanced.

Chapter 7 concludes this report by summarizing the major findings and proposals of the previous five chapters. For the reader in a hurry, or for the reader who prefers to know, as he reads, where the report is heading, Chapter 7 attempts to abridge the ideas in this document.

2
The growth of day care in Ontario: private demand and public subsidy

INTRODUCTION

It is no accident that extra-family child care has become in the last decade a matter of some public concern. There has been in recent years a dramatic increase in the number of mothers working and making arrangements for the care of their children. Quite naturally, there has been an expansion in the market for all types of child care, including, of course, institutional day care. The care of many children outside of the family has led to concern about the quality of care received by those children, and has raised the issues of public subsidization and regulation.

The formation of a rational public policy towards day care will be discussed in later chapters. It is the purpose of this chapter to give the reader a feel for the growth in recent years in both the private use of extra-family child care and the public involvement in the sector. Some of the issues dealt with later are raised in this chapter.

In the following sections I shall examine and attempt to explain the recent growth in labour force participation of mothers in Ontario and Canada look at the kind of arrangements these mothers have made for their children. Although much of the public dialogue has focused on formal day care centres, most children are cared for in informal arrangements. The growing government involvement in the child care sector is documented. Although day care has been regulated in Ontario since World War II, most of the increases in expenditures have taken place in the last ten years. Some explanations for that growth are offered. Finally, the survey is concluded by drawing together the insights and questions raised in the chapter.

INCREASES IN LABOUR FORCE PARTICIPATION OF MOTHERS

Women have been entering the labour force in large numbers since World War II. In recent years, the increase in labour force participation rates[1] for women has been due primarily to the influx of married women. And of primary interest to this paper, mothers have accounted for the largest increases among married women.

The numbers themselves can tell the story. Between 1964 and 1974, the participation rate of Canadian single women grew at a rate of only 0.7% per year[2] (from 48.3% to 51.9%). In the same period the participation rate of married women grew at a rate of 4.3% per year (from 24.1% to 36.7%). But, between April 1967 and October 1973, the participation rate of Canadian mothers grew at the much higher rate of 8.1% per year (from 21% to 35%).

Among mothers, the presence of preschool children does reduce labour force participation. However, the rate of increase in the labour force participation of mothers with preschoolers has been on the same level as that of other mothers. Table 1 shows participation rates for mothers in 1967 and 1973.

In absolute numbers, of the 1,238,000 working women in Ontario in 1973, 452,000 were mothers. Of these, 169,000 mothers had children under the age of six years, and 60,000 had children under the age of two (Statistics Canada, 1975, 33).

Motives for entering the labour force
The decision to work is generally examined by economists in the context of the trade-off for the consumer between income earned by working and leisure time forgone when work takes place. But for mothers, the choice is more often between working for income in the labour market and working within the household. The woman's decision to enter the labour force will be based primarily upon her relative efficiency in the market and the household. Can she earn enough to compensate for the loss of her productivity in the household – that is, can she earn enough to replace herself as child raiser[3] and to

1 The labour force participation rate may be defined as the percentage of a particular group that either holds a job or is actively seeking work.
2 In this case I mean by the growth rate of 0.7 per cent, that the *fraction* of women working increased by 0.7 per cent each year; that is, for example, out of a sample of 100,000 the number of working rose an average by about 0.7 per cent each year.
3 It is not meant to imply that only women engage in 'household production,' that is, care for children, clean house, cook, etc. Day care is talked about as a way to free *mothers* to work because in fact women are at present the primary care givers in most families.

TABLE 1

Growth of labour force participation of mothers in Ontario and Canada from April 1967 to October 1973, by school attendance of children

	Canada			Ontario		
	Participation rates (%)		Annual growth rate (%)	Participation rates (%)		Annual growth rate (%)
	April (1967)	October (1973)		April (1967)	October (1973)	
All women with children	21	35	8.1	25	40	7.5
Women with only full-time school children	28	42	6.4	32	47	6.1
Women with only preschool children	19	29	6.7	23	32	5.2
Women with both school and non-school children	15	26	8.9	19	30	7.3

SOURCE: May Nickson (1975), Table 5

compensate for the reduction in other household activities (cooking, cleaning, shopping, etc.)?

When we consider the recent and rapid movement of mothers into the labour force, the interesting question is not why it is happening, but why it has taken so long to happen. The economic history of industrialized nations tells a tale of the movement of most activities from the household or extended family into the marketplace. But child care has, until recently remained firmly with the household.

Consider the nature of production within the household. The care of several children uses only part of the time of a single adult, but requires full-time availability. So long as an adult's time is required for other household tasks, there is little point in contracting out for child care. Economists call this joint production. The 'cost' of an adult's time in the household is what the adult could earn by selling that time on the labour market. When joint production takes place within the household, each component of domestic production need bear only its 'share' of the total cost of time.

A number of factors have made the care of children for many women much more expensive in the home than in the market. One factor commonly mentioned is the increase in labour productivity and hence the wage rate. While important, the influence of higher wage rates in raising the opportunity cost of time used in the household is mitigated by the fact that extra-family day care, since it is extremely labour intensive, rises in price with the general wage rate.

Demographic factors have been influential. Women are now living longer and having fewer children than they did fifty years ago. In part, smaller families are a question of tastes – many families now desire fewer offspring. In part, it represents a reaction to decreases in child mortality. Fewer live births are necessary today to ensure (with some high probability) the survival to adulthood of some minimum number of children. And finally, the increased sophistication of family planning has made it more possible to reduce family size without taking extreme measures. In turn, smaller families make a permanent career much more attractive to many women, and this makes unattractive the interruption of that career during the child-raising years. The reduction in the number of children makes the 'cost' per child of the parents not working and staying at home much higher.

There have also been serious changes within the household. As smaller families have reduced the child care demands on the mother (while still requiring full-time availability), they have also reduced the demand for other household tasks (cooking, cleaning, laundering, etc.). Simultaneously, technological change in the household tasks has significantly reduced the amount of time necessary for their completion. Modern appliances (washing machines, dryers, dishwashers, vacuum cleaners, automatic stoves, etc.), permanent press fabrics, increased preparation of foodstuffs by supermarkets, the centralization of shopping in shopping centres, improved transportation, and so on, all make more and more of the time spent in child care less and less necessary for other tasks. Child care in the home becomes a less economical use of time.

Changes in attitude towards work by mothers has also been important. In the period immediately following World War II, a view generally held was that a woman's – and especially a mother's – place was in the home. It is now accepted that many women will want to pursue active careers and that those women may not wish, when they have young children, to discontinue labour force participation. Whether attitudes have followed or led economic trends is not clear. One might argue that the attitudes of the 1950s delayed the gradual increase in labour force participation that historically might have been expected. The rapid increase in the 1960s and 1970s thus might be a return to the long-run trend in labour force entry.

One final factor that must be mentioned is the increase over time of single-parent families. The division of labour in two-parent households in which one parent works and the other cares for children is impossible in the single-parent family. In 1973, there were over 80,000 unmarried mothers in Ontario. Their labour force participation rate was 57 per cent,[4] much above the 40 per cent rate for all mothers.

4 Communication from Statistics Canada on the Labour Force Household Survey of October 1973.

Predicting future increases in labour force participation is difficult. It is useful to note that holding the age of the youngest child in the household constant, the labour force participation rate rises as the age of the mother falls (Statistics Canada, 1975a, 84). If this reflects the fact that younger women view working mothers with more approval than do older women, it might suggest further increases in labour force participation in the years to come.[5]

THE CARE OF THE CHILDREN OF WORKING MOTHERS

The 452,000 working mothers in Ontario in 1973 had 895,000 children. The children of working mothers in Canada and Ontario are divided by age in Table 2. Not surprisingly, given the cost of care for younger children, most working mothers with preschool children had only one preschool child.[6]

Naturally all these children required care. In general, most have not been enrolled in day care centres; informal care, or 'care by kith,' has predominated. Day care has been growing rapidly, but some part of this growth has been induced by public funding. If those parents who receive no subsidy generally choose not to use day care centres when they work, then one should examine carefully a public policy on child care subsidies that directs most subsidies towards centres. In a later chapter, this argument will be developed, and it will be suggested that child care subsidies, if desirable, be directed towards the children of all working mothers.

What arrangements do working parents now make for their children? Two recent studies, one done in 1967, the other in 1973, provide this information.

The care of children of working mothers in 1967
The 1967 survey questioned working mothers about their child care arrangements.[7] Among the three- to four-year-old children of working mothers, almost half were cared for by relatives, a quarter by non-relatives, and only three

---

5 The data may also reflect the fact that older mothers have had a larger fraction of the total children they intend to have, and with larger families are naturally less inclined to work. Thus the 20-year-old with an infant is less likely to have older children in the household than the 35-year-old with an infant. In addition, the husband of the 35-year-old is more likely to have a higher income, decreasing the need for the woman to work.

6 Of the working mothers with preschoolers, only 23 per cent had more than one pre-schooler; of the working mothers with infants, only 4 per cent had more than one infant. Source: Statistics Canada, unpublished data from the Labour Force Household Survey of October 1973.

7 A number of serious questions have been raised about the accuracy of the 1967 data (discussions with John Buttrick and others), but the survey does provide us with some of our earliest information.

TABLE 2

Children of working mothers in Ontario and Canada in 1973,
by age group

	Total children	Children 6 years and over	Children 2-5 years old	Children under 2 years
Ontario	895,000	689,000	143,000	63,000
Canada	2,182,000	1,665,000	362,000	156,000

SOURCE: May Nickson (1975), Table 7

per cent by day care centres; the rest were cared for in a multiplicity of care arrangements or not at all (Women's Bureau, 1970, Table 23, page 41).

The overall figures can be misleading since child care arrangements will differ widely between mothers who work part time and those who pursue full-time work. In Table 3 (Appendix [8]) the care arrangements for preschool and school age children are presented according to the length of the mother's work day. In general, mothers working full time were more likely to arrange for paid care with non-relatives, and more likely to arrange for care by a relative who was not the child's father or older sibling. Care by fathers, older siblings, and the working mother herself becomes less likely when the mother works full time (the survey assumes that all non-relatives provide 'mainly paid' care, while relatives are 'mainly unpaid,' which need not be an accurate characterization).

For preschool children of full-time workers, care is most often provided by babysitters (non-relatives or relatives other than the father or sibling); all-day day care plays a minor role. For school age children, care by relatives is the usual arrangement. This is understandable, since public schools can care for children most of the working day. However, 'latchkey' children, who are uncared for between the end of school and the end of the mother's working day, make up a significant proportion of the total.

It is of interest to this paper that the 1967 survey appeared to find no increase in the use of paid arrangements (including day care) among mothers who worked full time. Table 4 shows the cost of child care in relation to the mother's earnings. Quite naturally, the amount spent on child care had a positive relation to the mother's income. But among those earning over $55 per week, which presumably includes most full-time workers, the use of unpaid arrangements is unrelated to income. Among families that did purchase care, the amount spent rose definitely with the mother's earnings. This might be

8 All remaining tables in this chapter are found in an appendix at the end of the chapter.

explained as follows: irrespective of earnings, working women prefer to have their children cared for by relatives. Only if this is not possible do women arrange for paid care, naturally spending more (buying 'better' care) as their incomes rise. This will be explained later in terms of lack of confidence in the operation of the free market, so that an arrangement with a trusted friend or relative is clearly preferred to the *quid pro quo* of the marketplace. Of course, the uncertainty about the quality of purchased care may be expressed also as an increase in the costs of information necessary to choose wisely, a factor that makes the non-market arrangement look more attractive.

The preference among working parents for care by unpaid relatives and trusted friends, even when income is not a barrier to purchasing higher cost high quality care, should make one suspicious of arguments that day care is the best way to care for children. In a later chapter it will be argued that child care programs that subsidize *only* care within day care centres are for the most part an inefficient high cost way to deliver high quality care to children.

It is also important to note the danger of using the distribution of past arrangements to predict the child care arrangements of new entrants into the labour force. The use of unpaid arrangements obviously depends upon the unpaid care-givers being available to the working mother. Since the availability of unpaid care makes the labour force participation more attractive to the mother, one might expect that mothers who are currently out of the labour force would have less access to unpaid care than those mothers who have already entered the labour market. This would suggest a greater dependence upon paid arrangements in the future if labour force participation rates for mothers continue to rise.[9] Furthermore, if extended families are becoming less prevalent, more working mothers will have to resort to the market to purchase child care.

Child care in 1973
The 1973 study indicates some information about changes in child care over time in Canada, as well as providing a check on the 1967 data. In addition, specific information about care in Ontario is available in the 1973 study. Tables 5 and 6 summarize the arrangements made by working parents for care of their preschool and school age children respectively.

The two studies are not strictly comparable. However, two time trends do appear to emerge. The first is that paid arrangements are becoming a more

9 Even more obvious is the fact that as participation rates of women continue to rise, fewer relatives will remain out of the labour force, thus becoming unavailable to provide unpaid child care. The breakdown of extended families would increase this tendency.

important component of child care arrangements, reinforcing the earlier comment that recent entrants to the labour force might have less access to unpaid care than those in the labour force for some time. Between 1967 and 1973 paid care as a percentage of all child care appears to have risen from 41 to 49 per cent.[10]

The second and stronger trend is the increase in the use of formal day care for preschool children in Canada, as a proportion of total care arrangements, from 2 per cent in 1967 to 7 per cent in 1973. The total number of preschool children cared for in Canadian centres grew from about 8000 in 1967 to 24,000 in 1973.[11]

The figures for Ontario in 1973 are very similar to those for the rest of Canada. Ontario has a somewhat larger percentage use of day care, due in part to demographic and economic factors (greater urbanization, higher wage rates, greater job opportunities), and in part to the active role of the Ontario provincial government in promoting day care.

For this report, special runs were done on the 1973 data for Ontario alone to examine the child care arrangements according to both mother's earnings and family income. Unfortunately, the small sample size for Ontario restricted the number of possible classifications. The results are shown in Table 7. It appears that an increase in mothers' earnings increases the use of paid care arrangements. The increase is small enough to be accounted for at least in some part by the fact that almost all part-time workers would be grouped in the 'earnings under $5,000' class. We cannot reject the earlier observation that an increase in wage rate may increase the amount spent on child care by those who make paid arrangements, but does not increase the number of paid arrangements made.

When family income (all earned and unearned income by all family members) increases, there seems to be no increase in the use of paid arrangements. This would support the hypothesis that working mothers prefer unpaid care by family or-friends when it is available. Among families with school children, paid arrangements decline when family income rises. It may be that the more affluent mothers with school children only work when they do not have to enter the marketplace to purchase care for their children, and can either arrange for informal unpaid care by friends and relatives, or can arrange their work hours to

10 Since the 1967 study assumed all care by relatives to be mainly unpaid and all care by non-relatives to be paid, while the 1973 study asked whether or not care was paid, the comparison is unreliable. The 49 per cent figure for 1973 is a weighted average of the two Canadian columns in Table 5.

11 This assumes that the studies are comparable and that the small numbers for day care in each case are statistically reliable. In that case, the number of children in day care grew at a rate of 18½ per cent per year.

eliminate the need to depend upon care by others. More affluent families may also delay labour force entry until school children are older (12 or 13 instead of 7 or 8) and less in need of organized care.

The 1973 survey also asked parents some questions in order to evaluate their child care. The answers, however, must be used with extreme care. In all cases, a majority of parents gave the most positive response. Moving from older to younger children, parents expressed both greater dissatisfaction with their care arrangements and greater difficulty in making those arrangements. Since the arranged care for younger children is of longer duration (older children are in school a good part of the day), and is seen by many to be more crucial to the child's development, neither result is surprising. But few parents are likely to announce that in order to work they have made poor arrangements for the care of their children. In addition, 'good,' 'fair,' and 'poor' depend upon the standards of the parents. Were parents comparing the child care arrangements with other care costing the same amount, or with some ideal high cost form of care? The questions and responses are shown in Table 8.

In perhaps the survey's most political question, parents were asked how their child care arrangements might be improved. The answers in Ontario were similar to answers in the rest of Canada. In general, mothers with school children only were more concerned about obtaining greater flexibility in work patterns (flexible hours, part-time work) than in altering their child care arrangements; the reverse is true for working mothers with preschoolers. In addition, proportionately more of the latter responded, indicating a greater desire overall for change among mothers with preschool children. The results are presented numerically in Table 9.

These results will be useful when we later discuss changes in public policy. Day care for school age children is very expensive. It will be suggested that the encouragement of flexible work hours might be of far more benefit to working mothers with school age children than the provision of day care. The overall satisfaction by parents with current care arrangements suggests that a policy of universal use of high cost institutional day care might not be the most efficient use of scarce resources.

The findings of both the 1967 and 1973 surveys are similar to those of equivalent studies in the United States (Emlen and Perry, 1974, Table 13, p. 104). Day care developed somewhat earlier in the United States than in Canada, though not earlier than in Ontario which has led the other Canadian provinces.

Day care surveys done by the Canada Assistance Plan
Three recent studies of day care centres done by the Canada Assistance Plan (CAP) show a rapid increase in formal child care facilities between 1971 and

1974 (Canada Assistance Plan, 1972, 1973, 1974). The total number of spaces increased at an annual rate of over 30 per cent between 1971 and 1973 and almost doubled between 1973 and 1974. This can be attributed not only to increases in private demand but also to significant shifts in government policy concerning the financing of day care services. Between 1974 and 1976 the growth of day care has been much slower.[12] We shall discuss in the next section changes in policy that have made available funds to support both the initial capital costs of setting up new centres and the ongoing expenses of providing day care to children. The CAP findings are summarized in Tables 10 and 11.

A number of noteworthy trends can be discussed within day care between 1971 and 1974. The first is the rapid growth in facilities for younger children, generally between the ages of 18 months and 3 years. To some extent, this growth has been induced by public subsidy. The particularly high cost of infant care (compared with care for older children) may make subsidies to these children an inefficient use of public funds in many cases. The second trend is the growing use of day care to supervise younger school children, about which a comment has been made above. The third is the rapid expansion of family or private home day care; that is, care of young children by an unrelated adult in a private home (and, for the purposes of the CAP studies, supervised by the Province or a formal agency). This is seen by many as a way to effect significant cost saving, a belief which will be discussed in detail later.

One should also note the trend towards larger centres (which shows up as an increase in 1973-74 in the average number of spaces per centre) and the trend towards the parent co-operative as a mode of providing day care. Parent co-operatives involve a majority of parents on the board of directors, and may also include parents participation in work in the centre itself; community board centres involve a majority of members on the board who do not have their children in the centre. Both parent co-operatives and community board centres are non profit.

Day care in Ontario
Ontario has led the rest of Canada in developing day care. In 1971 the all-day day care centres in Ontario comprised just under 80 per cent of all such centres in Canada. By 1974 the percentage was still over 40 per cent. The fall is the result of the emergence of day care elsewhere and not to a decay of day care in Ontario: the number of all day spaces in Ontario centres almost doubled

12 Most recent data provided by Howard Clifford to a Day Care Workshop, Queen's Park, 23 November 1976.

between 1971 and 1974. The growth of day care in Ontario from 1950 to 1974, with more detailed information for 1971-74, is shown in Table 12.

One must be careful in using blindly the numbers in Table 12 to indicate the use of day care centres by working mothers. For example, in 1973, there were over thirty-five thousand places for children in licensed nurseries or approved private homes. Yet the federal survey of working mothers discussed above estimated that just over ten thousand families in Ontario used day care centres or nurseries to care for their preschool children (Table 5). Even assuming more than one preschool child in some families, less than one-third of the available places are accounted for. This might suggest that the fraction of children of working parents receiving subsidy in day care could be much more than the fraction indicated in Table 12. In another study, John Buttrick estimates that one-third of the spaces in day care centres and nurseries in 1971 were used by working mothers.[13] The reason for this is that in 1971 and 1973 almost 60 per cent of the spaces in nurseries and day care centres were part time only, not meant for the working mother (although the percentage falls to 50 per cent in 1974 after significant growth in the sector). Some of the full-time spaces are used by mothers in school or by mothers who for some other reason (physical or mental disability, for example) are not able to care for their children. As discussed in Chapter 1, this report concentrates on day care for working women. However, when the best use of public subsidy is discussed in later chapters, emphasis will be placed on programs that reach all children in need irrespective of whether their parents work.

Examining more closely all-day day care centres in Ontario in 1973, one finds that Ontario still had most of the publicly owned day care centres in Canada: eighty-one of Canada's eighty-eight public centres were in Ontario. In addition, Ontario provided the lion's share of the all-day facilities in Canada for children under the age of three (2384 children under the age of two and a half cared for in Ontario, as compared with 3626 children under the age of *three* in all of Canada). A detailed breakdown of day care centres in Ontario in 1973 by sponsorship and ages of children is provided in Table 13.

The reader will notice that Table 13 also shows that the great majority of centres in Ontario conform to provincial norms, but that few are more generous in their staffing than the law requires. When regulation is discussed later in this paper, it will be argued that for various reasons the minimums set by provincial law tend inevitably to become the norms for most centres in the province.

---

13 John Buttrick, Table, 'Day care arrangements for children under 6 years, Ontario, 1971,' made available by the author (xerox).

Day care centres are distributed all over Ontario, although naturally they are concentrated in the larger cities – that is, the ratio of day care spaces to population is highest in urban areas. Data on the distribution of centres in Ontario by region are available from the author.

THE PUBLIC ROLE IN DAY CARE IN ONTARIO

The growth of day care in Ontario has been stimulated in no small way by the provincial government. As has become clear, the public purse subsidizes a significant fraction of the children in day care: from Table 12 it is evident that about 45 per cent of the all-day spaces in Ontario day care centres in 1974 were subsidized. It is useful to examine the development of present policy, and to understand what that policy now is.

Day care in Ontario up to 1966

The first day nursery in Ontario (the forerunner of the present Victoria Day Nursery) was founded in 1892 under the guidance of Hester How, but formal government involvement in day care did not emerge until World War II.[14] In 1926 the Institute for Child Study was founded at the University of Toronto under a Laura Spellman Rockefeller grant. The Institute proposed to introduce the developmental aspects of day care and began to educate parents and student teachers as well as carry out research on child development.

World War II represented a significant if temporary shift in the public view of day care. No longer a form of charity to poor children or as temporary help to damaged families, day care became a way to free badly needed mothers for work in essential industries. In March 1942 the Dominion-Provincial Agreement made available government subsidies, the costs of which were to be shared equally between Canada and the provinces, to provide day care for children. Day care was to be more than just custodial. It was also meant to include a developmental program for normal children. Ontario, however, was the only province to act under the agreement, setting up the Day Nurseries Branch within the Department of Public Welfare to administer the program. After one year, there were 30 new centres, an increase of 25 (Canada Council on Social Development, 1972).

The Canadian experience paralleled that of the United States, where the 1941 Lanham Act extended federal funding (on a 50-50 basis with the states) to day care under the Community Facilities Act. Many of the centres thus supported

14 This information along with some of the other facts in this section, come from the Canadian Council on Social Development (1972).

had been funded in the depression under Work Project Administration (WPA).[15] However, day care was viewed in both Canada and the US as an extreme wartime measure, not for normal use by mothers in healthy family situations. Although many other wartime programs continued after 1945, the end of the war spelled the end of federal support for day care. The Dominion-Provincial Agreement ended on 30 June 1946.

Mothers who intended to continue working after the war protested bitterly, resulting, in Ontario, in the Ontario Day Nursery Act in 1946, which offered 50 per cent funding of operating expenses to any municipality undertaking to provide day care. The act also required the licensing and inspection of day care centres and nursery schools. As our data on day care growth suggest, the response by the municipalities was not overwhelming (see Table 12: only 1147 children in Ontario in 1950 received subsidized day care). All municipal day care centres serving school age children closed down (there had been more than forty), and of almost thirty municipal centres for preschoolers, only sixteen were still in operation in 1947, most of them in Toronto.

Changes in the Day Nurseries Act: 1966 to the present
The Day Nurseries Act was not changed significantly for twenty years, during which time there was little growth in the number of publicly provided day care spaces. The new Day Nurseries Act of 1966, however, provided a major impetus for new centres by increasing from 50 to 80 per cent the share paid by the province of the operating and renovation costs incurred in municipal centres. Similar financing was extended to day care services purchased by municipalities from private day care centres for children of families in need.

In 1971 the Act was amended to extend the 80 per cent provincial financing to the purchase of services from approved homes. The same financing was also made available to approved local associations for the mentally retarded. More importantly for the growth of day care, the Day Care Amendment Act provided capital grants to municipalities and Indian bands of one-half of the costs of buying or building facilities for public nurseries or day care centres.

Shortly thereafter, in October 1971, the government of Ontario announced Project Day Care as part of its winter works program, allocating $10 million to create up to 150 new day nurseries serving up to 4000 new children (by the end of the project, something under 3000 new spaces were produced). The money was channelled into capital grants to pay for 100 per cent of all construction completed by 1 May 1972 (later extended to July), and provision was made to pay for 80 per cent of all work after that date.

15 For more details on the American experience, see Steinfels (1973).

In 1974 the Act was amended again to bring handicapped children under the Act in the same way as were the mentally retarded in 1971. The amendment also allowed the Minister to once again establish 100 per cent capital grants for new centres. On 4 June 1974, the Honourable Margaret Birch, provincial secretary for Social Development, announced the new program to the legislature (Birch, 1974). The program set in order three priorities for day care: first, more care for handicapped children; second, a commitment to serve low income families and native children; third, an acceleration of the growth of services to all children in Ontario. Fifteen million dollars was to be made available for three types of assistance: capital grants to municipalities and non-profit organizations to construct new centres, the grants to cover 100 per cent of the costs on all projects approved between 1 September 1974 and 31 March 1975; subsidies to the cost of day care for the handicapped to cover the high costs of care for these children; assistance to low-income families to be applied at any licensed day care centre in Ontario. The last provision bears some similarity to the voucher plan (or deinstitutionalization) often proposed in education.

Shifts in provincial expenditures
The provincial expenditures on day care reflect the changes in the legislation. Between 1949-50 and 1966-67 when the Act was changed, provincial expenditures increased by only 225 per cent (110 per cent when we account for inflation), from under $150,000 to just over $460,000. But between 1966-67 and 1970-71 expenditures rose by another 560 per cent to over $3,000,000, and by 1974-75, gross expenditures were over $16,000,000. The year-by-year record of expenditures is present in Table 14. The uneven growth between 1966-67 and 1974-75 looks considerably smoother when only operating expenditures are considered (that is, when the capital expenditures are deleted).[16]

The sudden shift in 1966 can be attributed not to an abrupt change in political thought at Queen's Park, but to the changes in federal legislation in that year. In 1966 the Canada Assistance Plan (CAP) reactivated the federal participation in funding day care by providing for equal sharing by Canada in the cost of providing day care to families in need (Hepworth, 1975, 135-139; Canadian Council on Social Development, 1972, 26-28). Initially, the federal government shared only in salaries for staff, but later changes extended financing to all day care costs (including capital costs). In general, therefore, public day care costs in Ontario are split among municipalities, the province, and the federal government,

16 The operating expenditures in millions of dollars on a year-to-year basis from 1968-69 to 1974-75 increase from 1.4 to 2.1 to 2.9 to 4.5 to 7.2 to 11.1 to 14.4, a remarkably steady growth.

with municipalities paying 20 per cent, the province 30 per cent, and Canada 50 per cent.

One might argue that Queen's Park has drifted into its current day care budget without any clear public decision to get into day care on a large scale. The open-ended cost-sharing provisions of CAP made the legislation hard to resist, and the municipalities, paying only 20 per cent, have been willing to go along, especially when faced with 100 per cent capital grants. The first capital program in 1971 seemed oriented more towards stimulating construction and the provincial economy than towards day care per se, but, of course, the centres once built led to greater operating expenditures. In 1975-76, severe limits have been clamped on provincial expenditures, terminating the open-ended nature of the Day Nurseries Act and reducing significantly the growth in day care.

The Canada Assistance Plan and day care
The design of provincial subsidies has been greatly influenced by the need to meet the requirements for cost-sharing under CAP (although Ontario's program could be more generous and still conform with CAP requirements).

The Canada Assistance Plan will share in day care expenses for families which, in addition to being in financial need, fall into one of the following categories: a single-parent family in which the parent is working, in school, undergoing medical treatment, or in a rehabilitation program; a two-parent family in which one parent is working and the other parent is working, in school, incapacitated, undergoing medical treatment, or in a rehabilitation program; any family for which a social welfare agency feels that day care will protect the child physically or developmentally or meet special needs of the family or the child. The definition of financial need is vague under CAP, and the province has laid out guidelines that have been adopted by the municipalities. Need is determined through the use of form 7 of the Ministry of Community and Social Services (a form that we analyse in some detail in later chapters). In brief, allowable expenses are subtracted from net family income. The form then subtracts 'exemptions' from the remainder. Any income remaining goes to pay for day care. The minimum fee is 25¢ per day. Exemptions include all family allowances, a fairly generous provision for contingencies (which for a family of five might easily run to $750 annually), and some municipally determined fraction of net earnings. This last fraction of earnings can be set by the municipality at its own discretion between zero and 25 per cent (until about ten years ago, the maximum exemption fraction was 10 per cent).[17] Ottawa and Toronto, like most other cities, use the 25 per cent exemption.

17 Information imparted verbally by the Ministry of Community and Social Services.

Under 1974 CAP guidelines, costs will be shared so long as provinces require either a needs test meeting the approval of the Department of National Health and Welfare (Ontario's test does) or an acceptable means (or income) test. While the needs test compares family income and assesses the parents fee on the basis of family income. If a means test, or fee schedule, is used, then families must begin to pay for day care once their incomes pass the provincial social assistance rates, and families must contribute at least fifty cents of every dollar earned beyond that point. No family with income above the provincial average (adjusted for family size) will receive any subsidy. Finally, under either a means test or a needs test, families not covered under the test must pay the full cost of day care, or that portion of the day care expenses which are not shared.

In Ontario, this latter provision has affected a number of districts, Ottawa and York-Peel in particular, which in the past have provided some subsidy to all users of municipal day care.[18] Each district is phasing out the subsidy.

Most provinces use the needs test. Income testing, where it has been tried, has proven to be less generous to many parents, necessitating the use of needs testing as a backstop.

Regulation of standards under the Day Nurseries Act
While public funding has influenced the rate of growth of day care, public regulation has had no small influence on the type of day care that has developed. The regulatory body, the Day Nurseries Branch, has been committed to encouraging and assisting in the upgrading of substandard facilities, to teaching centre operators how to improve standards, rather than to closing the centres down.

All day nurseries in Ontario require licensing under the Day Nurseries Act. A day nursery is defined as an institution caring for more than five unrelated children (under age ten) away from their parents for less than twenty-four hours continuously. The Act specifies standards for the physical layout of the day care centre.[19] Standards are also set for staff and program. Programs must meet specific scheduling requirements, balancing group and individual, indoor and outdoor, and active and quiet. Timetables and menus must be available in advance. The supervisor must have experience and special knowledge of preschool methods, and the staff must also have 'specialized knowledge' (Canadian Council

18 Information provided verbally by both directors.
19 Buildings must meet local health and fire laws, provide thirty square feet and two hundred fifty cubic feet of indoor space per child and specific outdoor play space fenced and properly supervised. Also required are more than one playroom for over twenty-five children, at least one toilet and wash basin for every fifteen children under age six, separate boys' and girls' toilets for children over age six, and specific arrangements for cots and personal equipment.

on Social Development, 1972, 123). There is some risk that trying to specify 'paper' qualifications for staff will raise costs without improving quality (disqualifying many potentially able staff who lack the qualifications), an argument examined in some detail in Chapter 6.

Perhaps the most important aspect of the Day Nurseries Act is its exact specification of the maximum child-to-staff ratios for different aged children. These ratios are presented in Table 15. Because the province subsidizes only day care with the maximum allowable ratio, and because even this care is very expensive for unsubsidized parents, few centres employ more staff than required by law.

In 1974 when the Honourable Margaret Birch announced the Day Care Expansion Project, she also proposed to increase the maximum child-to-staff ratios. Her proposal is shown in Table 15. The changes would have increased significantly the numbers of children cared for by the staff, from a 20 per cent increase for infants to a 50 per cent increase for five-year-olds in all-day programs. The government, faced with much opposition, has not implemented these changes.

Day care licences are renewed annually. Technically, failure to grant a licence or renewal can be appealed to the Day Care Review Board, established in 1970 to provide safeguards to the operators of day care centres. However, in only one case has the Ministry's denial of licence been overturned, and that case centred on the issue of zoning rather than on a fundamental objection by the Ministry to the nature of care provided in the centre.[20]

In contrast to day care centres, private-home day care does not require a licence. However, there is an implicit restriction on the number of children cared for by the 'day care mother,' since more than five children would constitute a day care centre under the Act. When public subsidy became possible for private-home day care in 1971, such care had to be approved to receive subsidy. Approval included inspection of the residence, medical examination, and supervision.

20 In fact, the Ministry had been required by law to insist on the fulfilment of local ordinances. We have no indication of whether the Ministry's true sympathies indeed may have been with the centre operator. This is not to imply that the Review Board has had no influence on the Day Nurseries Board, but rather to suggest that any influence has been informal and not through formal judicial decisions. In the most controversial case, that of the Sussex Campus co-operative (which was settled informally), the Review Board refused to accept a petition by parents and supported the Ministry's requirement that a director with suitable 'paper' qualifications be hired. Some of the background for this discussion stems from an interview with Don Bellamy, a member of the Review Board. I have devoted some time to this detailed discussion of day care regulations to anticipate some of our later discussion of public policy in this area.

CONCLUSION

Day care has grown rapidly in Ontario. This growth has been due, in part, to the private demand for child care arrangements for young children by their working mothers, whose numbers have grown dramatically. But the growth of day care has also been due to the public subsidies to the sector, both for capital expansion and for the yearly support of many of the children in day care (in 1974 almost half the preschool children in all-day programs received subsidy). And all-day care centres are carefully regulated by the province.

While this chapter has been largely descriptive, it has also introduced the crucial issues for public policy to be discussed later in this report. It is clear that day care reaches only a small fraction of the children of working parents. Those people in favour of more public spending on day care would argue that this small fraction proves that our programs are woefully inadequate, and that justice requires far more public involvement. Those against more public spending would argue that the government has blundered into an open-ended program whose eventual cost will be far beyond any present projections. The economist and this report will assume instead that the decision has been made on how much support to give to working mothers and their families. The question then becomes somewhat different. Do day care subsidies represent the most efficient way to use scarce public resources to reach and assist both children and their families? Given a certain level of public expenditure, how should a subsidy scheme best be designed?

Somewhat apart is the issue of regulation. It is clear that the Day Nurseries Branch is staffed by dedicated workers committed to improving day care. But economists are suspicious of regulation. Is the overall effect of regulation of day care desirable? Are there other methods that might better serve the public interest?

Before one can examine all these questions, it is necessary to have some feel for the costs involved in day care. That is the subject of Chapter 3. The remainder of this report will be concerned with the optimal design of public policy.

APPENDIX: TABLES

TABLE 3

Percentage distribution of care of children of working mothers, by hours of mothers' work, ages of children, and pecuniary nature of care arrangements, Canada, April 1967

Care arrangement	Total			1 to 24 hours		25 to 34 hours		35 hours and over	
	All ages	Under 6 years	6 years & over	Under 6 years	6 years & over	Under 6 years	6 years & over	Under 6 years	6 years & over
Total children (numbers in thousands) per cent	(908) 100	(357) 100	(551) 100	(103) 100	(141) 100	(30) 100	(48) 100	(224) 100	(363) 100
Mainly unpaid care									
Total	73	60	82	76	91	67	85	51	78
By father	22	16	25	32	33	20	35	9	21
With working mother	5	4	5	8	6	7	6	3	4
By a relative under 16	3	1	5	3	5	3	6	–	4
By other relative or household member (in home)	20	17	21	12	18	13	19	19	23
By a relative outside the home	4	8	2	7	2	7	–	8	3
Combination of 'in home' arrangements	9	8	9	8	10	13	6	8	9
No regular arrangements	10	4	14	7	17	3	13	3	14
Mainly paid care									
Total	27	41	18	24	9	33	15	49	22
By a non-relative in or outside the home	19	28	13	17	6	23	8	33	17
Day nursery/nursery school	1	2	–	1	–	3	–	3	–
Combination 'outside home' or 'other' arrangements	7	11	5	7	5	7	6	13	6

SOURCE: Women's Bureau (1970), Table 24, p. 42

TABLE 4

Percentage cost of care of children of working mothers in Canada in April 1967, by earnings of mother in week

	Earnings of working mother in reference week				
	All earnings	Under $25	$25-55	$55-100	$100 and over	No response
Total mothers						
(thousands)	(540)	(79)	(166)	(182)	(46)	(68)
per cent	100	100	100	100	100	100
Cost of child care in reference week (%)						
Nil	69	91	72	55	56	82
Under $10	10	8	14	9	4	4
$10-15	10	–	8	17	9	4
$15-20	6	–	4	10	9	6
Over $20	6	–	2	8	22	3

SOURCE: Women's Bureau (1970), Table 32, p. 50

TABLE 5

Child care arrangements made for preschool children in Canada and Ontario in 1973

Child care arrangement	Canada			Ontario
	Children in school part time	Children not attending school		Children not attending school
All families (numbers in thousands)	(190)	(347)		(129)
per cent	100	100		100
Work oriented arrangements (%)				
Mother works only when child in school	14	N/A		N/A
Mother takes child to work	3	5		5
Total	17	5		5
Unpaid arrangements (%)				
Care by person over 15 living in home	16	10		12
Care by sibling under 16	9	2		3
Care by neighbour, relative, or friend	19	18		17
Total	44	30		32
Paid care arrangements (%)				
Paid care in mother's home	14	21		18
Paid care in home of sitter	16	30		30
Day care centre or nursery	3	7		8
Total	33	57		56
Other arrangements	5	8		7

NOTE: Data on Ontario children in school part time not available
SOURCE: Statistics Canada (1975a), Table S-1.5, p. 87; the data from Ontario are unpublished and were made available by Statistics Canada

TABLE 6

Child care arrangements made for school age children in Canada and Ontario in 1973

Child care arrangement	Canada		Ontario
	Families with both preschoolers and school age children	Families with school age children only	Families with school age children only
All families (numbers in thousands)	(194)	(525)	(321)
per cent	100	100	100
Unpaid arrangements (%)			
Care by person over 15 living in home	14	17	19
Care by sibling under 16	–	6	6
Care by neighbour, relative, or friend	24	13	12
Total	42	36	36
Children care for selves			
Lunch at school	9	22	25
No lunch at school	–	23	20
Total	14	46	45
Paid care arrangements	33	11	12
Other arrangements	11	8	7

– means too small to be expressed.
SOURCE: Statistics Canada (1975a), Table S-1.7, p. 89; the unpublished data from Ontario were made available by Statistics Canada.

TABLE 7

Paid and unpaid child care arrangements in Ontario in 1973, by earned income of mother, by family income, and by school attendance of children under 16 years of age

	Child care arrangements	
	Unpaid (%)	Paid (%)
Children not attending school		
All children	34	57
By mother's earnings: under $5000	37	58
over $5000	*	69
By family income: under $10,000	*	29
over $10,000	62	61
Children attending school part time		
All children	61	34
By mother's earnings: under $5000	63	34
over $5000	*	*
By family income: under $10,000	*	*
over $10,000	59	35
Children attending school full day		
All children	72	17
By mother's earnings: under $5000	73	16
over $5000	71	23
By family income: under $10,000	68	22
over $10,000	73	17

NOTES: Unpaid care arrangements include both care by others, and child caring for self. All figures are rounded. In many cases small cell size makes the estimates unreliable. Because of other or no answers, rows add up to less than 100%. Because a significant number of families (up to 22% in one case) declined to provide family income or mother's earnings, or both, columns need not average out. An asterisk (*) indicates a cell size too small to report.
SOURCE: Statistics Canada, special computer run (#280) done for this project on data collected in the Child Care Survey, October 1973, Labour Force Survey

TABLE 8

Evaluation by working mothers in Canada in 1973 of child care arrangements by age of children (school attendance)

Mother's evaluation	Children not attending school (%)	Children attending school part-time (%)	School age children (full-time) (%)
A. How do you evaluate the child care arrangements reported above?:			
good	74	74	82
fair	19	22	15
poor	8	5	3
total	100	100	100
non-response rate	29	46	26
B. Over the past year, have you found it easy or difficult to make arrangements for the care of your children?:			
easy	68	73	81
difficult	32	27	19
total	100	100	100
non-response rate	13	17	19

SOURCE: Statistics Canada (1975a), Table S-1.9, p. 90

TABLE 9

Suggested methods of improving child care arrangement in Canada and Ontario in 1973

Suggestions for improvement (mother asked to choose best method)	Canada		Ontario		
	All working mothers	Women with school age children only	All working mothers	Women with school age children only	Women with preschool children
Changes in work patterns (%)					
Flexible working hours	25	34	27	37	17
More part-time work available	19	23	18	22	15
Total	44	57	45	59	32
Changes in child care (%)					
More day care centres	15	9	14	8	20
Approved register of sitters	14	10	14	10	17
Cheaper day care centres	11	5	10	6	15
Better location of day care centres	6	4	6	3	9
Total	46	28	44	26	61
Other Suggestions (%)	11	15	11	15	6
Total (%)	100	100	100	100	100
Non-response rate (%)	50	59	49	57	38

SOURCE: Statistics Canada (1975a), Table S-1.10, p. 91, with the addition of unpublished data on Ontario obtained from Statistics Canada.

TABLE 10

The growth of day care centres and spaces in Canada, by type of centre, and ages of children served, in the period 1971-74

	July 31 1971	March 31 1973	March 31 1974	Annual Rate of Growth (%)	
				1971-73	1973-74
Number of centres	682	971	1,528	24	57
Number of spaces					
Full day care (Group)	16,131	25,268	47,833	31	89
Lunch and after school	1,260	1,543	3,163	13	105
Family day care	–	1,562	4,185	–	168
Total	17,391	28,373	55,181	34	94
Children registered in day care					
Under age 3		3,626	11,351		213
Ages 3 to 5		22,074	38,952		76
Age 6 and over		1,773	4,878		175

SOURCE: Canada Assistance Plan (1974), Tables 1, 3, and 4 on pp. 2, 4, and 6.

TABLE 11

Sponsorship of centres in Canada, 1973 and 1974

Type of sponsorship	1973			1974			Annual rate of growth (%)	
	Number of centres	Number of spaces	Spaces per centre	Number of centres	Number of spaces	Spaces per centre	Number of centres	Number of spaces
Public	88	3,409	39	103	5,410	53	17	58
Community board	377	9,605	25	565	17,632	31	50	84
Parent co-op	43	1,245	29	179	6,509	36	316	423
Commercial	463	12,552	27	691	21,445	31	49	71
Total	971	26,811	28	1,538	50,996	33	58	90

SOURCE: Canada Assistance Plan (1974), Table 6, p. 8

TABLE 12

Children in licensed nurseries and approved private homes in Ontario, and number of children receiving public funds (full or partial subsidy) in Ontario, December 1950 to December 1974. Further Breakdowns for 1971-74

Year	Children in nurseries and homes	Children receiving public funds	Fraction of children subsidized (%)
1950	5,476	1,147	21
1951	5,956	1,147	19
1952	6,232	1,205	19
1953	6,588	1,201	18
1954	6,588	1,201	18
1955	6,781	1,104	16
1956	6,827	1,115	16
1957	6,797	1,115	16
1958	6,954	1,115	16
1959	7,279	1,104	15
1960	7,553	1,173	15
1961	8,528	1,148	13
1962	8,733	1,129	13
1963	9,458	1,115	12
1964	9,938	1,155	12
1965	11,034	1,882	17
1966	13,434	2,123	16
1967	18,350	2,099	11
1968	21,000	2,502	12
1969	26,150	3,786	14
1970	28,526	4,276	15
1971*	30,730	5,729	19
1972*	31,344	8,263	26
1973*	35,138	9,609	27
1974*	46,379	13,075	28

* In 1971-74, the following breakdown in nurseries and homes is available by part-day and all-day, and public (municipalities and Indian bands) and private (with percentage subsidized in brackets).

Type of centre	1971	1972	1973	1974
Public-All Day	4,265 (59%)	5,457 (66%)	5,828 (69%)	5,994 (75%)
Public-Part Day	831 (79%)	831 (79%)	851 (78%)	1,464 (50%)
Private-All Day	8,540 (25%)	8,272 (34%)	9,002 (35%)	17,033 (35%)
Private-Part Day	17,094 (7%)	16,784 (11%)	19,457 (9%)	21,888 (10%)
Total – All Day	12,805 (36%)	13,729 (47%)	14,830 (48%)	23,027 (45%)

SOURCE: Data made available in unpublished tables by Jean Stevenson, Assistant Director, Day Nurseries, Children's Services Bureau, Ministry of Community and Social Services, Hepburn Building, Queen's Park, Toronto, Ontario

TABLE 13

Full-day day care centres in Ontario, 31 March 1973

Sponsorship	Number of centres	Number of children					Staffing ratios		
		Under 18 months	18 months to 2½ years	2½ to 6 years	Lunch, after school	Total	Surpass provincial norms	Meet provincial norms	Below provincial norms
Public	81	59	427	2099	400	2985	25	56	2
Community board	70	126	418	1975	52	2571	11	56	4
Parent co-op	14	127	68	169	–	364	1	6	7
Commercial	120	212	912	3343	123	4950	5	99	13
Hospitals, student unions	2	13	22	43	–	78	0	2	0
Residential centres	14	–	–	128	–	128	0	14	0
Total	301	537	1847	7757	575	11,076	42	233	26

NOTES: 'lunch, after school' refers to day care programs organized to care for children in school full time, who still require care on holidays and at lunch and after school. 'Provincial norms' refer to legal requirements on staffing discussed below.
SOURCE: Hepworth (1975), p. 42

TABLE 14

Provincial expenditures in Ontario on day care, 1949-75

Year	Gross provincial expenditures on day care ($)	Percentage increase (%)	Year	Gross provincial expenditures on day care ($)	Percentage increase (%)
1949-50	144,476	–	1962-63	264,583	10
1950-51	197,913	37	1963-64	264,671	0
1951-52	217,537	10	1964-65	328,181	24
1952-53	216,868	0	1965-66	401,306	22
1953-54	212,527	–2	1966-67	466,805	16
1954-55	204,034	–4	1967-68	615,269	32
1955-56	196,166	–4	1968-69	1,570,147	55
1956-57	197,289	1	1969-70	2,220,255	41
1957-58	211,845	7	1970-71	3,083,166	39
1958-59	249,957	18	1971-72	8,083,253	162
1959-60	240,887	–4	1972-73	14,022,677	73
1960-61	230,832	–4	1973-74	11,712,645	–16
1961-62	240,826	4	1974-75	16,275,759	39

SOURCE: Unpublished data made available by Jean Stevenson, Assistant Director, Day Nurseries, Children's Services Bureau, Ministry of Community and Social Services, Hepburn Building, Queen's Park, Toronto, Ontario

TABLE 15

Current child-to-staff ratios specified by the Day Nurseries Act and Margaret Birch's proposed changes

Age of children and type of program	Maximum child-to-staff ratio in Day Nurseries Act	Changes proposed by Margaret Birch in 1974
General requirement	At least two staff in any day care centre	No change
Children under age of 18 months	3-1/3 to 1	4 to 1
Children between 18 months and 2 years of age	4-2/3 to 1	6 to 1
Children between ages of 2 years and 4 years		
(a) half-day programs	11 to 1	14 to 1
(b) full-day programs	8 to 1	12 to 1
Children 5 years old		
(a) half-day programs	22 to 1	no change
(b) full-day programs	11 to 1	16 to 1
Children between ages of 6 years and 9 years after school program	17 to 1	25 to 1

SOURCE: Margaret Birch (1974).

3
The cost of day care in Ontario

INTRODUCTION

In 1975 the cost of providing all-day day care for a preschool child (aged two to four years) in Toronto ran between $1800 and $2500. This single fact is at the heart of much of the public debate over day care policy. Because day care costs are a significant fraction of the earnings of the average worker, one might expect those costs to represent a major barrier to labour force participation. Because day care costs are somewhat less than the cost of welfare, day care subsidies to induce welfare mothers to work (and stop collecting welfare) are to some an attractive program. Because day care is expensive, any comprehensive public program providing care to all children would be a relatively high cost item in the provincial budget. Because day care is so much more expensive than most child care arrangements currently made by working parents (the average *paid* baby-sitting arrangement in 1973 in Canada cost about $1000 per year — see below, p. 53), one questions the efficiency of using subsidies that will steer parents towards the highest cost type of extra-family child care, unless it can be demonstrated that quality differences justify the additional cost.

This chapter will first examine the cost of different types of day care and attempt to explain both the magnitude of the costs and the apparent differences. Then proposals for reducing cost will be examined. It will become clear that the predominant factor in the costs of day care is the wages of those directly caring for the children. Cost differentials among centres are generally accounted for by different wage rates for the staff of those centres. It will be argued that proposals for cutting day care costs can be successful in the long run only by reducing the wages of day care workers – a difficult thing to do – or by reducing staff-child ratios and hence quality. It will be suggested that day care costs, even holding quality constant, will tend to rise in the coming years, especially if public subsidy increases.

Because of data limitations, the discussion is limited to day care in some of the major urban areas of Ontario. Lower wage rates outside the cities would bias downward day care costs in less urbanized areas, but transportation costs would generally be higher.

Day care costs within the municipal centres of Toronto, Ottawa and Peel are examined below, as are costs in private centres in Ontario. The possibility of reducing costs by cutting staff and the impact these cuts might have on the quality of day care being provided is considered. The actual expenditures of Canadian parents on extra-family child care with the formal day care costs developed in this chapter are compared, and private-home (or family) day care as an alternative to institutional day care is discussed. Finally, the costs of day care discussed in the chapter are summarized.

MUNICIPAL DAY CARE

As shown in Chapter 2, municipal day care (centres run by the municipalities) provides a significant fraction of the all-day spaces available in day care in Ontario (26 per cent in 1974). Most of the municipal day care is heavily subsidized, which in itself leads to problems, and in general, the cost of day care in Ontario is highest in the municipal centres. This has led to deep concern about ways in which public monies might be saved. In this section we examine the cost of municipal care and why it is so high.

The cost of one day of child care in 1975 in the municipal centres run by Metro Toronto was $12, expected to rise to between $13.00 and $13.50 in 1976.[1] In comparing costs among centres, it would be useful to compare the costs for older preschoolers (ages two to four years). The $12 per diem is an average over all children, including more expensive care for infants and less expensive care for school-age children. Using enrolment figures for the different age groups and making some assumptions about relative costs, one may estimate the municipal per diem cost for an older preschooler at $12.21.[2] Allowing for

1 Information provided in conversation with Marguerite Butt.
2 In March 1976, municipal centres in Metro Toronto cared for 123 infants (0-24 months), 830 preschoolers (2-4 years), 318 kindergarten children (5 years old), and 557 school children (6 years old and over). Assume that infants and toddlers under 2 years old cost approximately 2.9 times more than children aged 2 to 4 (Metro uses more staff to care for infants than is required by law); children age 5 in kindergarten cost approximately three-quarters of the cost of children aged 2 to 4; school children given care before and

absenteeism,[3] the cost for a 235-day year for a single child aged two to four years would be just under $2500 in 1975 and between $2700 and $2800 in 1976. In comparison, commercial centres in Toronto in 1975 charged about $1800 per year for the older preschooler.[4]

The city of Ottawa operates nine municipal centres. In 1975 the per diem cost was $10.48 for preschool and school age children (246 spaces) and $18.77 for infants and toddlers (44 spaces).[5] The costs for preschoolers seem similar to, if slightly below, the costs in Metro Toronto, while infant care is rather more expensive in Toronto, which does, however, use more staff than is required by Ontario law.

The region of Peel cared for 340 children in seven municipal centres. Peel reports that their per diem cost was $9.50 in both 1975 and 1976.[6] This seems quite low relative to Ottawa and Toronto, and indeed the quoted figure is unrealistic. In January 1976 true costs yielded an estimated per diem of over $15. Faced with intense local opposition, these high costs were cut towards a goal of $9.50 by increasing enrolments (reducing teacher/child ratios close to provincial minimums), by reducing teacher qualifications, and by effecting all other possible economies (maintenance, supplies, etc.). Even so, per diems were still running over $10 at the beginning of 1976, and Peel was considering a reduction in the number of centres operated.[7]

---

after school and during lunch cost approximately two-thirds of the cost of care for children aged 2 to 4. The relative costs for children under age 2 are derived by assuming that Metro uses adult-child ratios of just under 1:2 for this group (obtained from Mrs Adamson in Metro) and computing costs by assuming that direct staff costs account for 2/3 of the cost of care for a preschooler aged 2 to 4. Also assume that other costs are fixed, and that all staff receive similar pay. The relative costs for kindergarten and school age children come from the relative fees charged for these children in private day care centres.

3 In setting per diem costs for private centres from which Metro purchases day care, private centres are allowed to increase their daily charge to parents (paid whether or not the child is present, since parents pay on a monthly basis) by 15 per cent in computing the daily charge to Metro (paid only when the child is present). This assumes an absenteeism rate of 13 per cent (or 15/115). The Metro Toronto municipal centres per diem cost is thus the cost per day the child is actually present in the centre. Thus, in a 235-day year, the child is actually present only 235 x 0.87 = 204 days (assuming 13 per cent absenteeism).

4 Conversations with day care centre operators in Metro Toronto.

5 Data provided by Ottawa Regional Social Services, Day Care Branch, 495 Richmond Road, Ottawa.

6 James Crozier (1975) and telephone conversations with the Region of Peel and Mr Crozier on 11 March 1976.

7 Telephone conversations with James Crozier, 11 March 1976.

The three municipalities have had very different experiences with day care. In Toronto, parents who did not qualify for subsidy would be required to pay the full cost of care if they used the municipal centres. Partly because of this high cost (well above other centres), but mostly because these parents could not get their children into municipal centres (since priority was given to children in need), only about 3 per cent of the parents using municipal day care paid over $5 per day. Most paid virtually no fee (the minimum fee, whatever the needs test shows, is 25¢ per day). A majority (80 per cent) of the children in Toronto municipal centres come from single-parent families. The miniature ghettos created in the municipal centres can be cause for concern.

Both Ottawa and Peel have in the past charged less than full cost to all parents, regardless of income. In Ottawa the top fee in 1975 was $7 per day for residents of the municipality, while Peel had a top fee of $5 per day. In each case the significant subsidy paid to high income families using the centres con-travenes the regulations of the Canada Assistance Plan, and is likely to disappear. However, the across the board subsidy has led to a much more heterogeneous clientele in the municipal centres in Ottawa and Peel, as compared with Toronto. In Ottawa, in 1975, families paid the full fee for one-quarter of the children in full day spaces in municipal centres.[8] In Peel, where the maximum fee was even lower, 68 per cent of the families using municipal day care were two-parent families, and the average gross income of these families was $20,000. Using the needs test employed in Toronto, 72 per cent of the families would pay more than the $5 fee, and many would be required to pay full cost (Crozier, 1975). Whether these families *would* pay the higher fee, or would make alternate arrangements, is a matter for speculation.

But why is day care more expensive in municipal centres than in private centres? Because day care is extremely labour intensive, the explanation is most likely to be in the costs of staff. To give the reader a feel for the budget of a day care centre, Table 16 provides a three-year budget for one of the Metro Toronto municipal centres.[9] It shows that the wage and salaries and fringe benefits of staff involved in the direct care of children amounted to about 67 per cent of the total cost. Including casual and administration expenses, total labour costs account for 78 per cent, not including the labour inputs in other entries (laundry and main-tenance, for example). Food costs account for another 7.5 per cent of the total.

Metro Toronto municipal centre salaries are among the highest day care salaries paid in the province. Table 17 provides the salaries of those working in Toronto municipal day care centres in 1975, along with the composition of an

8 Data provided by Ottawa Regional Social Services, Day Care Branch, 495 Richmond Road, Ottawa.
9 In this chapter all tables are in the chapter itself rather than an Appendix.

TABLE 16

Costs in one Metro Toronto municipal day care centre, 1972-74

Item	Cost			
	Initial ($)	1972 ($)	1973 ($)	1974 ($)
Equipment-start up	16,267			
Alterations	24,165			
Salaries and wages				
Direct		86,270	91,707	99,146
Share of casual		6,816	8,034	9,894
Share of central administration		4,633	5,438	6,131
Total		97,719	105,179	115,171
Fringe benefits		8,902	9,582	10,180
Salaries, wages, and fringes		106,621	114,761	125,351
General				
Food		10,293	13,063	11,988
Heat, light, water		1,200	1,200	1,200
Household supplies and repairs		1,354	896	1,210
Equipment		154	504	1,080
Laundry		789	1,354	795
Playroom supplies		617	632	508
Rent		7,155	7,155	7,155
Maintenance		8,383	10,014	10,772
Sundry		1,415	916	598
Total		31,359	35,734	35,306
Grand total		137,980	150,495	160,657
Days care		14,730	14,935	14,688
Per diem rate		9.37	10.08	10.94

SOURCE: Commissioner of Social Services (1975). The centre is Edgeley Day Care Centre

average centre. The grade 2 day care assistant in Metro received between $7480 and $8445 per year in 1975 (compared with $7200 in Peel). In most private centres in Metro, the same position may have been paid as low as the minimum wage — about $5000 annually — and seldom over $7000 annually.

Yet, viewed in the context of the whole economy, even the salaries of municipal day care centre workers are hardly extraordinary. The wages are well below those of primary school teachers, for example (although levels of training are frequently different for teachers and day care workers). The grade 1 senior supervisor in the day care centre earned no more than $13,000, but might have responsibilities comparable to those of a principal of a small elementary school.

TABLE 17

Salaries in Metro Toronto municipal day care centres, 1975

Category	Annual salary without benefits ($)
Day care assistant	
grade 2	7,480- 8,445
grade 1	8,718- 9,628
Supervisor	
grade 1	9,955-11,102
Senior supervisor	
grade 2	10,790-11,992
grade 1	11,414-12,904

NOTE: An average centre serving 60 children aged 2-5 would
have: 6 Day care assistants grade 2, 3 Day care assistants
grade 1, 1 Day care supervisor grade 1. Senior supervisors,
grade 2, are required for centres serving aged 2-10. Senior
supervisors, grade 1, are required for centres serving infants
or more than 90 children.
SOURCE: Data received by phone from Mrs Adamson, in
the Child Care Branch of the Department of Social Services,
Metro Toronto

PRIVATE DAY CARE

To people with an ideological bias against public enterprise, the high costs in
municipal centres would come as no surprise. One obvious suggestion for saving
public money would be to return all care to the private sector where per diem
costs are significantly lower. In this section, private centres and their supposed
cost advantages are examined.

Despite an active public sector, most day care centres are privately owned
(more than three-quarters of the full-day centres, supplying almost three-
quarters of the full-day spaces in 1974). These private centres can be commercial
(for profit) or non-profit. Among the commercial centres are many small single
proprietorship centres, and some larger corporations with a number of separate
centres centrally controlled. The commercial centres may be genuinely concerned with earning profits, or may be run by individuals deeply committed to
quality day care who take lower profits (or none at all) in order to improve
programming in the centre.

In general, fees in 1974 ran around $150 per month for preschool children
(ages 2-4 years). This is well below the costs in municipally run day care centres.
In fact, the municipalities already purchase day care spaces (for those in need)
from the private centres, both commercial and non-profit. These private centres

also sell care to the public. The commercial centres are constrained not to charge more to the municipalities than is paid by unsubsidized families. Non-profit centres, which frequently sell care below cost because they can raise funds from other sources (charitable donations), must justify the per diem charge to the municipality.[10] But a close study of these centres and their costs would suggest that eliminating municipal centres and expanding the purchase agreements with private centres would not save money in the long run.

In 1975 the Metro Toronto Department of Social Services collected cost data from all the private day care centres with which the Department had arranged purchase agreements. Most of these centres agreed to allow the Department to release these data to this project.

The data yielded a number of interesting results, the most obvious of which is that day care costs are extremely variable. Only centres that handle preschool children and no infants were examined. Forty non-profit centres (including three co-operatives) had an average per diem cost of $8.44, but the variation around that mean produced a standard deviation of $1.96 (that is, you would expect only about 68 per cent of the observations to lie within one standard deviation of the mean – or between 56.48 and $10.40). Thirty-eight commercial centres had an average per diem cost of $7.67, with a standard deviation of $1.15. Overall, the seventy-eight centres had an average per diem cost of $8.06 and a standard deviation of $1.78.

The differences in costs among centres can be explained in a number of different ways. In considering whether the increased use of private centres for subsidized children would reduce public expenditure, it is most interesting to note that the variation on costs seems to be related to the fraction of children in a centre receiving public subsidy. The municipality contracts with each centre to support certain children in the centre with full or partial subsidy. For centres with a higher fraction of subsidized children, per diem costs appear to be higher. To test this, a simple regression was run with one independent variable – the percentage of subsidized children in the centre (or PCS) – and one dependent variable – the per diem cost in the centre (or CPD). The regression was run separately on non-profit and commercial centres, and then on all centres to-gether. The results of the various runs are shown in Table 18.

In general, there was a significant relationship between the two variables. The R^2 statistic was between 0.22 and 0.27 for all runs, which means that about one-quarter of the variation in per diem costs can be 'explained' by variations in

10 In calculating the per diem costs, the municipalities do not allow for the cost of staff who exceed the minimum provincial staff-to-child ratios, nor, for example, is the cost of social work counselling accepted.

TABLE 18

Results of regression of per diem costs in private day care centres on the percentage of children in a given centre subsidized by the government

Sample	Number of observations	Estimate for α	Standard error for α	Estimate for β	Standard error for β	R^2
All non-profit centres	40	6.40	0.62	0.0360	0.0098	0.26
Non-profit centres, excluding co-operatives	37	6.42	0.64	0.0346	0.0105	0.24
Commercial centres	38	6.25	0.47	0.0284	0.0088	0.22
All centres	78	6.18	0.39	0.0352	0.0067	0.26

NOTE: The equation being estimated, by ordinary least squares, is

$$CPD_i = \alpha + \beta(PCS_i) + \mu_i,$$

where CPD_i = Cost per diem for preschool children ages 2 to 5 in the ith centre (only centres with preschoolers are included), measured in dollars,

PCS_i = Percentage of children receiving public subsidy in the ith centre,

α, β = coefficients to be estimated,

μ_i = Error term.

SOURCE: Data collected for the author by Department of Social Services, Metropolitan Toronto.

the percentage of children. In all cases, the coefficient on PCS was significant at the 0.1 per cent level. For non-profit centres alone, a rise of ten percentage points in the percentage of children subsidized (as from 40 per cent subsidized to 50 per cent subsidized) would raise the per diem by an average of 36¢ (35¢ if the three co-operative centres are deleted). For commercial centres alone, a rise of ten percentage points in the percentage of children subsidized would raise the per diem cost by an average of 28¢.

The reader is urged to interpret these results with great care. The immediate conclusion that springs to mind is that economists who warn about the inefficiency of government vis-à-vis the market are right. Non-profit centres are run by individuals who usually are deeply committed to the concept of high quality day care. The fewer children in the centre whose parents must pay full fee, the more standards can be raised (more expensive equipment, more highly trained and higher paid staff, etc.) without eroding the clientele (as costs rise, parents leave the centre and make other arrangements). In commercial centres, this tendency is more limited. Profit rates are restricted to 10 per cent of costs, but many centre operators are genuinely committed to quality. Furthermore, profits can be disguised as allowed costs (for example, rent on a building owned by the centre operator, or the operator's salary, since in many centres the owner may also be the supervisor). In any case, the absence of 'market discipline' when the government subsidizes most children removes the need for the operator to control costs, quite aside from quality and profit.

There are, however, several other possible explanations of the relationship between costs and the percentage of subsidized children. First, labour costs are a major component of day care costs, yet the workers are generally poorly paid. Part of the reason is the reluctance of many day care workers to demand high wages when those costs must be passed on directly to the parent in higher fees. Day care workers are often persons committed to the concept of day care and sympathetic to the working mother. And on a more pragmatic level, day care is already costly, and higher wages and fees would likely drive many day care users to employ alternate arrangements, and might well close some centres. But when the public treasury bears much of the cost, these concerns are minimized, and labour tends to be more insistent on its wage demands.

Second, many of the individuals working for the municipalities, who choose the centres with which purchase agreements are concluded, are themselves committed to quality day care. They naturally choose the best centres, being particularly careful where the number of subsidized children is high. Once the centres are chosen, the municipality naturally aids the centre to improve its program, once again concentrating on the centres with the most subsidized children. In fact Metro Toronto was actively engaged in encouraging the private centres, with which they entered into agreements, to upgrade standards of care. This process has been halted by provincial spending ceilings.[11]

Finally, it may well be that a higher proportion of subsidized children raises the per child costs necessary to ensure an adequate program. Subsidized children are from poorer homes, many from single-parent families, and some from multiple-problem families. One must remember that subsidized day care serves not only working mothers, but also families in which parents are alcoholic or otherwise mentally ill, where children are in day care because it is the healthiest situation possible. To serve these children, especially in a centre where they are concentrated, may well involve higher costs.

The statistical analysis in Table 18 is also flawed by the fact that data are available only for centres that have at least some subsidized children, that is, centres that deal with the Department of Social Services. The majority of centres do not sell spaces to the city, and hence are not in the sample.

It should not be surprising that only about one-quarter of the variation in the per diem costs can be explained by variations in the proportion of subsidized children. Many other factors explain the different costs in different centres. There is a high variation in the value of services provided free or at reduced cost to the different centres. These include low rental arrangements in public or semi-public buildings, donated toys and other supplies, labour at below market wages (especially in religiously oriented centres), volunteer labour, etc. For example, five non-profit centres had per diem costs under $6.00. All five appear to be religiously oriented, and thus may be the beneficiaries of low-wage workers from religious orders. The variation in rent is also striking. Among non-profit centres, about 20 per cent had virtually no accommodation costs, while another 30 per cent had accommodation costs of over 10 per cent of their total budget.[12]

In addition, in a rapidly growing sector like day care, there is apt to be significant variation in the ages of the various centres. Centres started in the last several years have staff that have not (by definition) been with the centre for long, relative to the staff of older centres. The newer staff is generally paid less, if only because there is little time to have accumulated increases for merit, experience, etc.

Figures on private centres in Ottawa undertaking purchase of service agreements with the municipality reinforce the conclusion reached about Toronto centres. Although there are too few centres to run extensive regressions, as in the

11 Conversations with the Department of Social Services, Metropolitan Toronto.
12 Examining the percentage of a centre's costs that went to cover the building (or accommodations), I found for non-profit centres a mean of 6.6 and a standard deviation of 5.26.

case of Toronto, per diem costs vary widely and are correlated with the proportion of children in a centre who are subsidized.

In summary, one might expect that a major shift of subsidized children from public to private centres would not save anywhere near the amount of money suggested by the current differences between average per diem costs in the two kinds of centres. As more children in private centres are subsidized, costs inevitably begin to rise.

One can also suggest that current per diem costs are an inaccurate guide to day care costs in the future, *if* a major expansion in public day care subsidies is contemplated. Increased public involvement is likely to speed unionization of day care workers and raise their wages significantly. In fact, the highest paid day care workers are in the municipal centres, unionized in the Union of Public Employees (CUPE), although even they still lag behind comparable public sectors. Furthermore, low wages are due in part to the youth and hence disorganization of the industry. The expansion and stability brought on by massive public subsidy would lead inevitably to higher wages and costs. Obviously, wages would have to rise to attract new workers into the sector if major expansion occurs.

Even without expansion of public subsidies, the cost of day care may be expected to rise somewhat faster than the general rate of inflation in years to come. This is because day care is so labour intensive, and wages tend to rise faster than prices.[13] Costs would remain stable only if productivity gains could compensate for higher wages. But productivity gains would imply that one adult is somehow able to care for more children. The 'care' in day care is a very personal relationship between the care-giver and the children for whom he or she is responsible. More children per adult would seem inevitably to erode this relationship. In this sense, day care is one of those commodities that must rise in price over time. Baumol suggests that activities may be roughly divided into two classes: those in which labour is an instrument in attaining the final product, and in which rapid productivity increases can occur; and those in which labour is for practical purposes the end product itself, and in which productivity increases come slowly if at all (Baumol, 1967, 415-17). Day care would seem clearly to lie in the second class.

This is not to suggest that publically supported day care should not expand. It is, however, suggested that expansion in the future is likely to involve per diem costs significantly above those in existence today.

13 Between 1964 and 1975, prices rose by approximately 77 per cent, while average hourly earnings in manufacturing rose by approximately 151 per cent. Source: *Bank of Canada Review,* December 1975, Table 61, 'Consumer price index' and Table 62, 'Other prices and costs.'

INCREASES IN CHILD-STAFF RATIOS AND THE QUALITY OF CARE

Most of the cost of day care is in salaries. The lower per diem costs in private centres compared to municipal centres are due largely to the lower wages of private day care centre workers, a condition one might expect to change if subsidized children were all transferred into private centres. As was suggested above, if wages continue to rise, costs can fall only if child-staff ratios increase, as suggested by Margaret Birch in 1974. Can one comment upon the impact on quality of child care were such a change to take place?[14]

The quality of day care is dependent upon many factors, not the least of which is the particular characteristics of the workers in a particular centre. But over the sector as a whole, it is clear that quality of care is highly correlated with the staff-child ratio. Staff cuts should not be viewed lightly. One study of day care quality and staff ratios was done in the United States in 1967 by the Department of Health, Education and Welfare (HEW). The cost of care was considered for two groups of children. The first group was comprised of pre-school children aged three to five years who were cared for in the centres for full days. The second group was composed of school children between the ages of six and fourteen years, cared for before and after school (U.S. Department of Health, Education, and Welfare, 1967). The costs and staff-to-child-ratios are summarized in Table 19. The qualities of care are defined in three ways: 'minimum' care is defined as 'the level essential to maintain the health and safety of the child, but with relatively little attention to his developmental needs'; 'acceptable' care is defined as 'to include a basic program of developmental activities as well as providing minimum custodial care'; and 'desirable' care is defined as 'to include the full range of general and specialized developmental activities suitable to *individualized* development' (HEW, 1975).

---

14 In fact, some significant differences do exist already among child-staff ratios in Ontario day care centres, although the variations are nothing like the changes proposed by Margaret Birch. This occurs because of an ambiguity in the Day Nurseries Act. The Act specifies that one adult must be present for every eight children aged two to four years in a full-day program. Metro Toronto's municipal centres interpret this to mean one adult for every eight children enrolled in the centre. With the predictable absenteeism of 10 to 15 per cent each day, this means that the children present often receive more intensive care, with ratios averaging one adult for every 6.8-7.2 children present. But many private centres interpret the legislation as requiring one adult for every eight children in attendance on any given day, allowing the centres to over-enrol by some fraction of the anticipated number of absentees, so that there is closer to one adult for every eight children present on any given day.

TABLE 19

United States Department of Health, Education, and Welfare; Day care estimates: Annual
cost per child and staff per child, 1967

I Preschool children (3-5) in a centre for a full day

	Quality level		
	Minimum	Acceptable	Desirable
Annual cost per child	$1245	$1862	$2320
Staff per child			
(a) Classroom professional	1/20	1/15	1/15
(b) Classroom non-professional	2/20	2/15	3/15
(c) Social service professional	1/150	1/100	1/100
(d) Community, parent, health aides	0	1/100	2/100
(e) Business and maintenance	2/100	3/100	3/100
(f) Special resource personnel	1/300	1/100	2/100
(g) Supervision	1/100	2/100	2/100

II School age children – before and after school and summer care

	Quality level	
	Minimum	Acceptable-desirable*
Annual cost per child	$310	$653
Staff per child		
A School year (3 hours per day)		
(a) Day care workers	1/25	1/15
(b) Special resource personnel	0	1/45
(c) Business	1/250	1/250
(d) Supervision	1/250	2/250
B Summer period (12 weeks)		
(a) Recreation supervisors	1/25	1/15
(b) Special resource personnel	0	1/30
(c) Business	1/250	1/250
(d) Supervision	1/250	3/250

SOURCE: United States Department of Health, Education, and Welfare (1967)
*No differentiation in HEW tables between Acceptable and Desirable for school age
children.

The HEW report went on to comment:

Individual experts will differ as to the elements required for each level of quality. Most experts feel that the disadvantages to children of a 'minimum' level
program far outweigh the advantages of having the mother work. Some will feel
that for children from 'disadvantaged' homes only the 'desirable' level is appropriate. The figures shown represent a consensus among a number of experts of
what would be required at each level of quality. (HEW, 1967)

The HEW figures do not seem out of line with the costs derived by other American studies, which may, of course, have been influenced by the HEW results. For
example, Mary Rowe examined cost studies done by Abt Associates (1971) and
Westinghouse (1970), and after correcting the numbers to standardize cost
measurement, found that their cost estimates compared with those of HEW
(Rowe, 1971).

Comparing the standards of the Ontario centres with those set by HEW, it
appears that the level of care in Metro Toronto centres is on a level with or at
most only slightly above 'minimum' care. The Toronto centre for sixty preschool children described in Table 17 had six grade 2 day care assistants, three
grade 1 day care assistants, and one grade 2 supervisor. The 'minimum' centre
described by HEW, serving sixty children, would have six classroom non-
professionals, three classroom professionals, 0.4 of a social service professional,
and 0.6 of a supervisor (the latter two tasks might be assumed to be taken care
of by the one Ontario supervisor). In fairness, it should be noted that the HEW
'non-professionals' are more poorly trained than the grade 2 day care assistant in
Toronto. In addition, Toronto public day care centres must expend additional
resources dealing with children from multi-problem families (families requiring
day care for reasons other than the parents' participation in the labour force —
for example, families in which alcoholism or mental illness is a problem).

The 'acceptable' HEW centre serving sixty children would have eight classroom non-professionals and four classroom professionals, along with 0.6 of a
social service professional, 0.6 of a special resource person, and 1.2 supervisors.
This would raise the staff-child ratio from 1:8 to approximately 1:5½. The
reader might note that although more staff are hired, the day care 'day' is longer
than eight hours, so that to maintain a given number of staff throughout the
day, approximately 25 to 30 per cent additional staff must be hired.

The 'desirable' HEW centre serving sixty children has twelve classroom non-
professionals, four classroom professionals, 0.6 of a social service professional,
1.2 special resource people, and 1.2 supervisors. This raises the staff-child ratio
to approximately 1:4¼.

The cost of 'minimum,' 'acceptable,' and 'desirable' care in Ontario today can be estimated only by assuming some level for the salaries of the day care workers. Using the Metro Toronto salaries in municipal day care centres, assuming 10 per cent fringe benefits, and using the general rule of thumb that salaries for direct care-givers account for about three-quarters of the cost of care in 'minimum' centres, 'minimum' care would cost about $2400 per year per child in 1975, just under the cost of care in Metro centres. 'Acceptable' care would then cost about $3500 per year per child, and 'desirable' care about $4300 per year per child. Using the lower salaries in private centres, the costs would be about 20 per cent less.

One thing that does stand out in the HEW study is the relatively low cost of care for school age children, compared with the higher relative costs in Ontario. In the HEW study, the cost of 'minimum' care for the full year for school children ran about one-quarter the cost of 'minimum' care for older preschool children; in Ontario the ratio of costs is closer to two-thirds. One partial explanation is that the Ontario children are younger and require more care: the HEW figures are for care for children aged 6 to 14 years, while Ontario considers only care for children under 10 years old. The Ontario staff-to-child ratios for school children are much closer to what HEW would call desirable than to minimum care. Much of the difference, however, is explained by the fact that HEW was examining care that was very different from that currently provided to school age children in Ontario. In the US, most children eat their lunch at school. The day care program would provide children with care in their regular schools for about an hour before school and several hours after school (although, of course, during summers and school holidays, full-day supervision is required). The use of existing school facilities would cut rent to zero, reduce significantly many building- and facilities-related expenses (such as equipment, supplies, maintenance), and cut travel costs. In Ontario, on the other hand, school children are cared for in separate day care centres before and after school and during lunch. It will be argued later that institutional changes, both in work hours, and in the use of schools could significantly reduce the cost of providing quality day care to school age children.

In examining the whole issue of quality, it must be pointed out that the HEW study represents the views on quality of only one group of experts. Clearly, many day care professionals might disagree with the statement that with the care provided by municipal day care, 'the disadvantages to children far outweigh the advantages of having the mother work,' to paraphrase the HEW conclusion (HEW, 1967). Provincial Secretary Margaret Birch even felt justified in proposing a 50 per cent increase in the number of 3- to 5-year-old children cared for in the current centres (changing the ratio from 1:8 to 1:12). The author, as an economist, is not qualified to decide. The point that should be made, however, is that while day care in Ontario is indeed very expensive, it is not clear that costs can be cut without serious implications for the quality of the care provided. And truly high quality care might well be much more expensive.

ALTERNATIVES TO DAY CARE: CAN PRIVATE HOME DAY CARE
REDUCE PUBLIC EXPENDITURE?

Day care, even in the lowest cost private centres, still costs far more than the arrangements made by the majority of parents who make alternative paid care arrangements for their children. In the absence of subsidy, few parents are willing to pay the cost of institutional day care, especially the even higher costs of municipal day care, as some municipalities have found when they have been forced to charge full cost to parents not in financial need.

The 1973 Statistics Canada day care survey (discussed in Chapter 2) asked parents in Canada the amount they paid per week for child care. The results are summarized in Table 20, which includes only parents who actually paid for care. Only 13 per cent spent more than $26 per week on care, and most of those did not use day care. It is interesting to note that in fact the average cost of day care paid by parents in Canada was not much different from the cost of other kinds of care. This can be explained by the high rate of subsidy given to much of the day care purchased in Canada.[15] It can also be noted that the most expensive care on average was in the parent's own home. A number of explanations for this can occur. Care in the home might involve more children, including part-time casual supervision of school-aged children. In addition, the paid care-giver in the child's home frequently has other tasks (house cleaning, laundry, preparing supper).

Since babysitting arrangements cost less than the full cost of institutional day care, one attempt to lower public costs has been the introduction of supervised private-home day care. It is felt that reductions in costs of capital and administration can result in lower per diem costs. The evidence is not yet conclusive. In Ottawa, the per diem costs for private home care averaged about $8.65 for full-day care in 1975, not significantly less than the per diem in the day care centres (of course, depending upon the number of infants served, costs saved could be significant). In Toronto, much of the subsidized private home care is administered through voluntary agencies — out of a total of approximately 425 children in subsidized private-home day care in January 1975, the Toronto

15 There are also problems with the data. If a working parent had the child cared for at no cost by a relative, supplemented by nursery school (which is much less expensive than full-day day care), then this would be the cost entered as day care in Table 19.

TABLE 20

The percentage distribution of the cost of child care for parents using paid arrangements for children not attending school, Canada, 1973

Cost of care per week ($)	Type of Arrangement				
	Care in parent's home (%)	Care in home of sitter (%)	Day care centre (%)	Other arrangements (%)	Grand total (%)
1 – 5	8	6	9	21	8
6 – 10	12	16	9	24	14
11 – 15	14	32	12	21	23
16 – 20	23	23	35	24	24
21 – 25	21	14	23	9	17
26 and up	23	8	12	3	13
Average cost per week	$21.95	$17.59	$19.21	$13.50	$19.01
Median cost per week	$20.00	$15.00	$20.00	$13.00	$15.00
Number responding	288	476	94	34	892
(Non-response rate)	(19%)	(5%)	(7%)	(75%)	(18%)

SOURCE: Statistics Canada, unpublished data from the Labour Force Household Survey of October 1973. Small cells are prone to statistical error

Department of Social Services were responsible for only 50 (Metropolitan Toronto, 1975). For the children administered by the voluntary agencies, per diems charged to Metro Toronto ran about $8.00 in 1974 and almost $12.00 in 1975 (Metropolitan Toronto, 1975).[16] These figures may be somewhat misleading. The agencies frequently handle children 'at risk' who require additional assistance. The agencies also may be absorbing some expenses in their own budgets. And the $12.00 figure is an estimate (the 50 per cent increase in one year is unusual).

One agency – Family Day Care Services – which administered a significant fraction of the private-home day care for the municipality, made available a breakdown of their costs.[17] The per diem cost for a preschool child in 1975 amounted to just over $10.00, which compares well with the per diem cost in Metro Toronto municipal centres of $12.00 for children aged 2-4, and of substantially more than $12.00 for infants. The $10 cost is not, however, below the cost of day care in most private centres.

Private-home day care does not appear to have realized the initial hopes that significant reductions might occur in the costs of administration. Almost six supervisory visits to a day care home each year, along with significant new recruitment of homes each year, have raised administration and supervision costs, to over one third of the total per diem cost. Moreover, the major saving in infant care (over the day care centre) is achieved by paying day care mothers no more for infants than for older preschoolers. This implicitly assumes that infants require no more care than older children. Yet the provincial regulations on staff-child ratios in day care centres require higher ratios for infants, which would seem to indicate that infants do need more intensive supervision.

In fact, the major saving in private-home day care is the lower salary paid to day care mothers relative to full-time employees in day nurseries. A day care mother caring for five preschool children over the age of three years in her home (the maximum number of children allowed under the law) would have received $31.50 per day in 1975, which is $7387.50 over a two-hundred and thirty-five day year. The mother receives no fringe benefits, no sick leave, and loses $31.50 every day she cannot work. She gets no paid vacation (other than the normal vacation days during which the parents of the children do not themselves work.) The mother works more than eight hours a day, and must also pay for

16 In 1974, a total of $479,000 went to private agencies which provided care for 284 children in January and 344 children by December. In 1975, an estimated $858,000 went to the agencies, caring for 344 children in January (Metropolitan Toronto, 1975).
17 Family Day Care Services (1974), and information obtained in an interview with Miss Sheila Tee, Director of Child Care Services, 8 August 1975.

food, supplies, equipment, maintenance, and any wear and tear on her home out of that total. Not surprisingly, the agencies advise many private-home day care mothers to deduct up to 90 per cent of their income as expenses on their income tax. Of course, mothers may care for less than five children, but their remuneration then drops accordingly.

Compare this situation to the *starting* salary of a Metro Toronto public centre worker: $7500 per year, plus benefits, sick leave, paid vacation (2 weeks), and no 'expenses.' Once again we may expect the growing public involvement in private-home day care to lead to demands for an upgrading of 'worker' salaries to 'reasonable' levels (perhaps accompanied by the organization of day care mothers into a union or its equivalent). This would in turn effectively eliminate any cost advantages of private home day care over institutional day care centres.

This last point may be seen by consulting again the HEW study cited earlier which also examined the costs of minimum, acceptable, and desirable family day care (private-home day care). Day care mothers caring for five children (four for acceptable and desirable care) were paid on a par with day care centre workers, and allowances were given for food, supplies, utilities, equipment, and so on. The costs of the three qualities of care were $1423 for minimum, $2032 for acceptable, and $2372 for desirable family care (HEW, 1967). In each case, family day care cost more than care in a day care centre: 14 per cent more for 'minimum' care, a smaller percentage more for higher quality care.

Why then is babysitting in the free market so much cheaper than day care? This, after all, is the main reason that private-home day care looked initially like an economical alternative. The very informality of the babysitting sector keeps costs down by avoiding any interference with low wages by unions, minimum wages, and requirements for paid vacations, sick leave, and so on. And of no small importance, the informality allows for some tax evasion by the care-giver by providing for at least some payments in cash. However, the unsupervised nature of these arrangements, which is what keeps down costs, is exactly what raises the most serious questions about the quality of care and the safety of the child, an issue to which we return in a later chapter.

The cost advantages of private-home day care would seem to be theoretically non-existent under current law. Any gains from reducing administration and capital costs would be outweighed by the lower number of preschoolers that may be cared for by one adult (five in the private home as against eight in the centre), unless salaries were much lower in private-home day care than in the centres. Since day care is a labour-intensive industry, with limited opportunities for true productivity gains, savings can only be achieved in the cost per child by lowering the staff-child ratio or lowering the wages paid to day care workers.

There is unfortunately no 'free lunch' (that is, no way to cut per diem costs without hurting someone).

SUMMARY

In municipal day care centres in which most children are subsidized, day care in 1975 for a child aged two to four years cost about $2500. Day care in many private centres ran about $1800 during the same period, but one can be sceptical as to whether money can be saved in the long run by a transfer of subsidized children from municipal to private facilities. It appears that per diem costs rise when there are more subsidized children in a centre. In some ways this is to be expected. Costs are higher in public centres mainly because salaries are higher, since day care is labour intensive, and salaries are higher because public day care workers are unionized and because the government can pay higher wages, while unsubsidized parents (through their day care fees) will not. The problem is not necessarily eliminated by moving all subsidized children into private centres.

The same problem emerges in the use of supervised private-home day care to save costs. Day care mothers are as likely to unite to demand higher fees from the government as are workers in day care centres. Already the per diem costs in private-home day care do not represent a substantial saving.

Proposals to reduce staff-to-child ratios would save costs, but the implications for quality are substantial. Already provincial centres would be judged as only 'minimum' by at least one US study.

4
Optimal subsidies to day care: a theoretical approach

As the previous chapters have shown, the recent growth in the number of day care centres has been induced at least partially by public subsidies. The high cost of a day care space raises the obvious issue of whether these subsidies represent the most efficient use of public funds. At the same time, of course, a number of people argue that day care subsidies must be much more extensive to be effective. Many recent discussions of the demand for day care begin by listing the total number of children under age six with working mothers (or who might, in the future, have working mothers).[1] The Canadian Council on Social Development (1972, iii) defines 'potential demand' for day care as 'demand for the service from people who, given changed financial or social circumstances, or if a different type of service were available, might express a demand for the service.' The Report of the Royal Commission on the Status of Women in 1971 (cited in the Canadian Council on Social Development, 1972) estimates a need for 450,000 day care slots in the years to come. This assumes that all children of working mothers should be in day care centres, which, given the cost of day care, assumes extensive subsidies to the centres.

The debate is further complicated by the fact that the advocates of increased subsidy form a coalition of diverse interests, with component subgroups supporting

---

1 See, for example, Hepworth (1975), p. 13. There are many less formal studies which take the same approach, for example, the Social Planning and Research Council of Hamilton and District (1971).

very different goals and types of programs. Women's rights supporters argue that children are mainly the responsibility of the general public and not of the individual parent, and that free universal day care is essential for the emancipation of individual women. Believers in early education argue that the early years of a child's life are crucial, that high quality day care is essential to the development of most children whose mothers work and is beneficial to many children now cared for at home by their mothers. Welfare administrators concerned about rising costs suggest that day care might save the government money by assisting welfare mothers to work.

It is clear that the decision to expand day care subsidies is more than just an issue of economic efficiency. The subsidies represent a significant redistribution of income in society, from taxpayers in general to families with young children. If all families have the same number of children, to some extent this just spreads out over time the costs of children — parents receive subsidies when children are young, and when their children grow older, parents pay for the subsidies to the children of other parents. But since taxes rise with income, and not all adults have children, and since many times the subsidies go only to families in particular income classes, the distributional impact of the program cannot be dismissed so easily. This redistribution of income, implicit in most day care proposals, is partially what makes day care a highly ideological issue.

While this report will not ignore the redistributive aspects of day care, the primary concern will be the design of programs that best use the resources available to assist both the poor and children in general. Is public day care necessarily the best way to assist disadvantaged children and their families? Could these same monies be used more efficiently to help the poor? Do day care subsidies meet industrial needs for female workers[2] (or, conversely, can the labour market absorb the potential entrants)? How should subsidies best be directed in order to reach the families most in need without resulting in perverse behaviour by the people in question?

We can state this last point in terms of economic efficiency and equity. It would be inefficient to induce all women to use day care for their children and enter the labour force, independent of the woman's productivity and the costs of day care for the woman's children. It would be inefficient to structure programs to assist children so that women must work in order that their children might participate. It would be inequitable to penalize the children of low income women who do not work. It would be inequitable to direct high quality day care to poor families and leave the children of the near-poor in inadequate care. It

2 Work is ongoing on this point by Eilene McIntyre, in her doctoral thesis for the University of Toronto School of Social Work.

would be inefficient to transfer all children of currently working parents into high-quality high-cost day care when many of those children are presently cared for at much lower cost and with equal care and affection in informal arrangements.

In this chapter, the theoretical justifications for day care subsidies are examined. For analysis, these justifications are divided into two classes. In the first class are all arguments that day care subsidies are an efficient way to increase the well-being of families, where that well-being is measured by the adults in the family (henceforth for 'well-being' the micro-economic term 'utility' will be used). In this class of arguments, subsidized day care enables parents more easily to work (increasing family income). Children may also be better off under the subsidy, and this in turn increases family utility, since parents are interested in the well-being of their children. But children are seen as the concern primarily of parents. If children are not well off, then in this view of the world the problem is that their parents are also not well off.

The second class of arguments includes all those that treat children quite apart from their parents as a clientele for services. This can occur only by assuming that the government values the utility of children more than do the parents of the children. For, if the government values children as much as do the children's parents, then parents will transfer exactly the same resources as would the government, and the government might just as well transfer resources to the family as to the children themselves. In this case the government may wish to transfer resources directly to children to make them better off than their parents may intend.

The division is arbitrary, since many arguments for day care subsidies aim at both helping parents and enriching the lives of children. But the division allows some strong conclusions. Insofar as the aim of policy is to help families, it will be shown that only limited subsidies to day care are justified. This generally means a maximum of deductibility from earned income before taxes are assessed or welfare payments computed. Insofar as the aim is to help children, further subsidies can be justified, but only if those subsidies reach all children in the target population – a position that will imply subsidies to more than day care alone.

The chapter begins by considering day care subsidies when the goal is to help families. A detailed mathematical model to prove some of the points in this section is developed in the Appendix. Then the discussion turns to an examination of child care subsidies to reach children as a separate concern of policy. Some other motives for subsidizing day care are touched on briefly, while the final section summarizes some of the conclusions of this chapter. Particular programs will be considered in Chapter 5.

DAY CARE TO HELP FAMILIES

(a) *General arguments*

Consider first the arguments that day care is an efficient way to assist families with young children. It may be argued that the presence of young children has a severe financial impact on the family. If the children are cared for at home, the family must do without the earnings of the mother (or the adult who cares for the children) during a period when expenditures are apt to be higher than normal. This is an even more serious problem in a single-parent family. But even if public policy deems assistance to the family to be necessary, one must ask if that assistance should take the form of a subsidy to day care.

It is relatively straightforward for the economist to show that in the absence of other distortions, a transfer of dollars is always superior to a transfer of the equivalent resources 'in kind' (that is, a transfer of goods directly to the family). Given $2400 in cash instead of $2400 worth of day care, the family is free to purchase the same day care. Thus, if the family chooses an alternative use for the $2400, the family is clearly better off. Since the government pays out the same money (in this case, $2400), it should also prefer the cash transfer, since it increases the family's utility.

This simplistic argument is not applicable simply because 'other distortions' are not generally absent. In the case of day care, the most important 'other distortion' is the tax on earned income. If the family above takes the $2400 in day care, the mother will work and pay taxes on her earnings; if the family takes $2400 in cash and purchases other goods, the mother frequently will not work and will not pay taxes. The government – and other taxpayers – do not consider these two alternatives to be equally desirable. It may be argued that in many cases the $2400 in day care will increase tax revenues by more than $2400, saving the government money.

This last point is especially true for families on welfare who face a high (in fact, close to confiscatory) marginal tax back rate on earnings,[3] since their benefits fall rapidly as earned income rises. Thus, day care is seen as an efficient way to save welfare dollars, as the following editorial in *The Toronto Star* would suggest:

---

3 The tax back rate on the welfare recipient measures the reduction in government benefits when earnings rise. Thus if the tax back rate (also called the benefit reduction rate) is 75 per cent, a one dollar increase in earnings decreases benefits by seventy-five cents, and the wage earner gains only twenty-five cents for every dollar earned. The tax back rate functions for the welfare recipient much as the marginal tax rate does for the income earner not on welfare. Later on, the term 'tax rate' in the model will be used to refer to the tax back rate on families receiving benefits as well as to the normal tax rate on taxpayers.

Day care, on which Queen's Park was dragging its feet even before austerity set in, is another service Metro is considering cutting back. It's hard to see that there will be economy here. Mothers who can't work if they can't find day care for their children will end up on welfare — and that could cost the taxpayers more than providing day care.[4]

To see this clearly, a numerical example will be useful. Imagine a single-parent family that receives $4000 annually on welfare. When the parent works, this payment is reduced by three-quarters of the amount earned over $1200. Thus, yearly earnings of $4800 would reduce welfare payments from $4000 to $1300, a reduction of $2700 (three-quarters of $3600). The family has one preschool child whose day care would cost $2400. Suppose, first, that day care is not subsidized. If the parent can earn $6000 a year, work looks unattractive. When the parent works, welfare falls to $400 (the reduction of 75 per cent of $4800), and disposable income, after paying for day care, is $4000. The parent will stay at home and collect $4000 welfare.

In this case, subsidized day care would seem to make obvious sense. The parent would receive free day care, would work, and would have a disposable income of $6400 ($6000 plus $400 in welfare), a gain to the family of $2400 over welfare. The government would pay out $2400 for day care and $400 for welfare, a gain of $1200 over the situation in which the family receives full welfare.

However, while this example demonstrates that day care subsidies may in many cases be superior to no subsidy at all, it does not demonstrate that day care subsidies are the best of all policy alternatives. Consider, for example, the alternative policy for this family of simply reducing from 75 to 25 per cent the marginal tax rate (or, in this case, the benefit reduction rate or tax back rate) on earnings over $1200, leaving day care unsubsidized. If the parent works, welfare benefits now fall by only $1200 (25 per cent of $4800), and disposable income, after paying for day care, is again $6400 and the total cost to the government is again $2800. One reason the two policies appear so alike is that a subsidy to day care functions very much like a wage subsidy, the parents net wage from working being simply total earnings minus taxes (or reductions in benefits) minus payments for day care.

Subsidizing day care increases the net wage, and so exactly does reducing taxes (or reducing the amount by which benefits are cut when income is earned). But the day care subsidy involves other inefficiencies not present in the tax

---

4 *The Toronto Star,* Editorial, 'Metro Budget, Taking Food from the Poor,' Saturday, 10 January 1976, p. B2.

reduction. First of all, the day care subsidy can apply to families where day care is clearly inefficient. Consider a family in which there are three preschoolers aged one, three, and four years. Day care in a Metro Toronto municipal centre for all three children would cost upwards of $10,000. If the mother can earn only $6000 when she works, it is hard to argue that day care represents an efficient use of public funds, yet subsidized day care would make work an attractive proposition. A reduction of the marginal tax rate, even to zero, would not induce this mother to work.

Secondly, subsidizing day care itself implies that this is the most desirable way to care for children when their parents work. But it is clear that most parents who now work and who are not subsidized do not choose day care. These families prefer care given by a relative or friend and, if this is not possible, favour paid babysitting. A subsidy for the use of high-cost day care may induce many parents to use day care over a lower cost, reliable alternative. Suppose, for example, a parent has available babysitting in the home of a trusted friend, and both agree that $25 per week would represent a fair price. If subsidized free day care is offered to the family, most families would choose to use it, at a cost to the public of far more than $25 per week.

It has been shown that although subsidizing day care is often desirable, given a high tax on earnings, it is frequently more efficient simply to lower that tax rate. It has not been shown that all subsidies to day care are inefficient. A subsidy to day care can induce parents to use better day care, and this, in turn, may make work more attractive and increase tax revenues. The argument is somewhat complicated and is developed in the next section.

(b) *The optimal day care subsidy: an economic exercise*
Partial subsidies to day care need not face the inefficiencies mentioned earlier in this section. Suppose, for example, that expenditures on child care are made deductible from earned income before any taxes are assessed and before any reduction in welfare benefits is computed. If child care expenses exceeded the parent's earnings, then the parent would receive no immediate financial gain by working, avoiding the first inefficiency discussed above. And since all child care expenses are deductible, no special incentive exists to use higher-cost day care over lower-cost, reliable care arrangements.

But why would such an arrangement be superior to reducing the tax rate on earnings? The answer requires a fairly sophisticated economic model developed in the Appendix. The model assumes that each household maximizes some utility function which depends upon the household's enjoyment of both adult activities and the raising of children. Both adult activities and child-raising require not only goods and services purchased in the marketplace, but also time to use and enjoy these goods and services. The model assumes that the adults in the household may divide their time among three choices: they may sell some time in the marketplace to acquire money to purchase goods and services both for themselves and for their children (of course, any other monies possessed by the household are used the same way); they may use some time in child-raising; they may use some time to employ and enjoy the goods and services purchased for their own use. Given the prices of time (that is, the after tax wage rate) and of the goods and services used for themselves and for their children, the household will be able to determine the most efficient pattern of work in and out of the household.

The demand for day care emerges from the model as part of the demand for goods and services for children. As more time is sold in the marketplace – that is, as the parent works in the labour force – less time is available for child care, and the parent naturally replaces that time with services purchased in the marketplace – that is, some kind of extra-family day care. The model asks under what circumstances increasing the rate of subsidy to day care will be more efficient than simply reducing the tax rate on earnings.

To answer this question, a tax rate on earnings and a subsidy rate towards the purchase of 'children's goods' are introduced into the model. As the subsidy rate is increased, the tax rate is also raised so as to leave unchanged the utility of the family. The optimal combination of a tax rate on earnings and a subsidy to day care will be the one that maximizes the well-being of the government; that is, that maximizes net tax revenues from the family (the difference between tax revenues from the tax on earned income and government expenditures towards the purchase of day care).

The reader interested in theory is referred to the Appendix at the end of this chapter. For the more policy-oriented reader, the strong conclusion of the model may be fairly easily stated. Economists have long understood that different goods might optimally be taxed at different rates. Under certain assumptions, some subsidy to the purchase of child care can be justified. But that subsidy should be for only a fraction of the expense of child care, that fraction not to exceed the tax rate on earnings. More simply expressed, the maximum subsidy to child care that can be justified in order to assist a family is the deductibility from earnings of child care expenses (as discussed above).

(c) *Day care as investment in women*
It may be instructive to apply the theory that has been developed so far to an argument frequently made for subsidized day care. If women with children are absent from the work force during the children's younger years, then the mothers lose their skills, and re-enter the labour force at an older age, competing

with younger workers, and having missed opportunities for promotion. This increases well above the current wage rate the value to the family of having the parent work when children are young and explains in part why, in fact, many young parents do work when the net take-home pay, after deducting taxes, work expenses, day care, transportation, extra clothes, and the loss of home production, is very low — or even negative. To illustrate this, consider the loss of income in present value terms when the parent remains out of the work force for one year. (We may assume the decision to work must be made anew each year.) Suppose that real wages rise by the fraction a (100a per cent) for each year that an individual is in the labour force, but that an individual's real wage declines by the fraction b for each year the individual stays out of the labour force. If the wage in the initial year is w_0 and the discount rate of future real income is r, and we assume forty more years in the labour force, then the loss in real present value caused by the parent not working for this year is

$$\text{Loss} = w_0 + w_0 \frac{a+b}{r-a} \left[1 - \left(\frac{1+a}{1+r}\right)^{40} \right].$$

Assume $r = 0.05$ and $a = 0.03$, then the real loss in not working is above this year's wage by 107 per cent if $b = 0.01$, and by 134 per cent if $b = 0.02$. The reader may work out the loss for other values of r, a, and b.

It might be argued that for many low income families wage rate increases due to experience are low, as is any decay in skills and employability. This would make a and b close to zero and reduce the loss to the current year's wage. But whether the loss is large or small, the benefits of continuous work in the labour force all accrue to the parent. The term w employed in the model in the Appendix could be inflated to account for these benefits, and the model could still not argue for subsidies to day care beyond tax deductibility.

In fact, the problem might be expressed in terms of a failure in capital markets. In a perfect world, mothers could finance today's day care by borrowing against tomorrow's higher income. Since this is impossible, long-term government loans would be the theoretical solution. A practical solution is not to subsidize high cost day care, but to lower drastically the tax rate faced by parents with young children (perhaps even to the point of paying wage subsidies), financed (if, in fact, it loses revenue) by higher taxes on parents in later years.

Although the argument is stated in economic terms, the same results apply when the argument is phrased in more psychological terms: it can be argued that removing a parent from the work force and placing the parent on welfare when children are young destroys the individual's connection to work as a way of life.

When children grow older, the individual no longer feels able to work, and remains on welfare forever. In the model above, the individual would perceive b, the decay in work skills, to be larger than it really is. Even if this were true – it is, after all, an empirical question – the answer would be lower tax rates on parents with young children, not subsidies to day care.

(d) *A summing-up*

This report is not hostile to the particular problems faced by families with young children. At a time when finances are low, the greatest demands are placed on the resources of the family, including the parents' time. But whatever role public policy chooses to play, the maximum subsidy to day care itself is deductibility. Even if the government were to assume full financial responsibility for children (as proposed by some groups), universal free day care would represent an inefficient use of resources. Far superior would be a combination of cash transfers to the family and a reduction of marginal tax rates on the parents' earnings.

DAY CARE TO HELP CHILDREN

It has been established that deductibility is the maximum subsidy that should be provided to day care, under the assumption that the goal of public policy is the maximization of family (parental) utility. Of course, public policy also views children as a separate clientele from their parents. Seen as individuals, rather than as inputs into their parents' utility function, children might be felt to be deserving of a level of well-being above that decided upon by their parents. This is not a new suggestion. Child welfare laws have generally intervened when alcoholism, mental illness, family breakup, drug addiction, or accident have endangered children's well-being. And, of course, health legislation (immunization, dental care) and educational requirements intervene in more prevalent but less exceptional circumstances. It would not be an enormous leap to suggest special attention to the developmental needs of preschool children.

A number of justifications might be offered for treating children as separate from their parents. It may be argued, for example, that expenditures on children involve significant externalities.[5] This is an argument frequently made to justify public education. 'Properly' brought up children benefit not only their own parents but everyone else in society. Parents considering only their own children will tend to under-spend on education and development, imposing costs on the rest of society. Children who grow up uneducated and uncared for require

---

5 An externality occurs when consumption by one individual affects the well-being of other consumers.

significant public expenditures on welfare and crime prevention, thus reducing the general quality of life for all citizens. Public policy, aware of these externalities, might seek to influence families to divert more of their resources towards children than those families might otherwise tend to do (the suggestion that they were not sufficiently concerned about their children would most likely horrify many parents). Since it is impossible to identify and subsidize the time parents spend with children, governments subsidize the purchase of goods directed towards children.

This argument may be put another way. The inadequately cared for children themselves might prefer more resources devoted to their care. But, of course, preschool children can not borrow against future earnings to finance their own day care, nor can their parents pledge the future income of the children against current loans to finance child education. This would argue for subsidies to child care, but not necessarily to the children of poor working parents only. In fact, this argument is often put in terms of investing in the future of society. Dollars spent on children may return many times the initial investment in terms of developing more productive, healthier adults in the future.

Of course, adults now in a situation of poverty are a concern for society. But public policy might wish to limit its support for poor adults, feeling that the desire to redistribute income must be tempered by the need to retain suitable incentives for self-betterment. At the same time, valuing equal opportunity in society dictates a somewhat greater concern for directing public monies towards the children of the poor. This is already one justification for the expenditure of public funds on education. The possibilities of effective intervention when children are even younger make additional expenditures a possibility.

In this sense, child care subsidies may be seen as a social insurance scheme into which children are imagined to enter before they are born. Unsure of the status or resources of their parents, these children want to protect themselves against ending up in too disadvantageous a situation.

Even if it is decided that public policy would favour increasing the utility of young children beyond that planned by their families, there is some debate over whether or not this is possible. In the United States, this debate centred on the evaluations of Headstart, a short-run early education program designed to give better preparation to poor children for participation in public school. The original evaluation of Head Start, undertaken by the Westinghouse Learning Corporation and Ohio University, branded Head Start a failure (see Cicirelli et al., 1969). Although the report found some initial improvement in the performance of the Head Start children when compared with that of a control group, the improvement died out as the children progressed through school. Several years after public school began, no significant difference was found between the performance of Head Start children and those in control groups.

The evaluation evoked significant criticism (for a flavour of the debate, see Smith and Bissell, 1970; Cicirelli, Evans, and Schiller, 1970; Light and Smith, 1970). Besides some criticism of the methodology and statistical techniques of the Westinghouse-Ohio study, the critics argued that the interpretation given the results was misleading. Since the Head Start program frequently took place only the summer before children entered public school (although there were some full-year programs), and since the children had just returned to neighbourhood schools after Head Start, it is hardly surprising that many of its effects wore off after several years. In fact, the program could be viewed as a success. That Head Start had some impact in the first year of public school is significant, given the short duration of the program. The wearing off of the improvement should indicate not failure but the need for follow-up programs for the Head Start children in the summers following the later grades of school.

Furthermore, critics argued, Head Start was an experimental program spread over the country, so that some of its programs would naturally be more successful than others. Lumping all the nation's Head Start programs together, finding no significant overall long run impact, and rejecting the whole program, is missing the very important lessons that can be learned from the differences among the programs themselves.

Discussions with day care professionals in Canada reveal that they are positive about the impact of day care on the future well-being of disadvantaged children.[6] The economist cannot make that judgment. It is possible to assert that full-day day care may not be the most efficient way to use resources to reach children. Enriched day care for all children would be extremely expensive, and, moreover, implies that it is desirable to remove all children from their homes for eight to ten hours each day. Would a shorter enriched program be more efficient?

If day care is not fully subsidized, then a program for children emphasizing partially subsidized day care would clearly miss most children, including children whose parents did not work — few non-working parents would absorb even a fraction of the cost of full-day, enriched day care — and children whose working parents chose low cost alternatives to day care. In Chapter 5 a voucher scheme will be proposed to reach all children in the target population.

DAY CARE AS PATERNALISM

A final set of motives for subsidizing day care would fall under the general category of paternalism. For one reason or another, the poor (or parents in general) are not acting as some feel they 'should.' Public policy is seen as a way

6 For example, Howard Clifford, in an interview in Ottawa, 25 November 1975.

to impose certain behaviour patterns on these people. In one version of this argument, taxpayers prefer to give money to the poor in the form of day care in order to induce those on welfare to work, even though this may involve a greater level of public expenditure to achieve the same level of household utility of those on welfare. The argument is one of 'donor's preferences.' Donor's preferences argues that optimal policy ought to consider not only the welfare of the recipients of public monies, but also the preferences of taxpayers for the uses to which poor recipients put that money. The author, following Mishan, believes that this argument has no proper role in public policy.[7] However, whatever considerations the economist believes are important, it is clear that politicians are responsive to the wishes of taxpayers. As far as day care is concerned, these wishes are contradictory: on one side, there has been a desire to keep mothers at home with their children; on the other side, there has been a desire to put those on welfare to work. Shifts in the balance of these two views have had much to do with the making of day care policy.

It can also be argued that some significant portion of the population do not know *how* to care for their children. It is not that parents desire less utility for children than would society (as suggested earlier), but rather that some parents do not know how to maximize that utility. Children would be better off in day care centres, cared for by experts. Again the economist can say little about this argument, except that it raises serious legal and ethical questions.

Finally, a justification advanced for publically supported day care is the desire to change the basis for child raising from the nuclear family to the extended community. Since this is an attempt to induce voters to undertake politically what they could do individually (but do not), the liberal economist has little useful analysis to offer.

CONCLUSION

This chapter has attempted to prove several general propositions about child care subsidies. The first is that if subsidizing child care is seen as a way to help

7 For part of the debate on donor's preferences, see Hochman and Rogers, 1969; Musgrave, 1970; Goldfarb, 1970; and Mishan, 1972. Mishan argues that welfare economics ought to be based on ethics, and not accept externalities based either on benevolence or malevolence as agenda for society.

  Even if one accepted donor's preferences, there would seem little of value that the economist can say in discussing their application to public policy. Economics would seem most useful in identifying ways to be efficient. A conscious decision to sacrifice efficiency for other goals is clearly possible. The economist can do little but point out the costs of such actions.

families, then the maximum efficient subsidy is the deductibility of child care expenditures before taxes or welfare benefits are computed. If it is desirable to help the family further, a reduction in the tax rate (even below zero; that is, to the point of subsidizing the wage rate) is far superior to a day care subsidy.

The second proposition is that further subsidies to child care can be justified by a desire to reach children as a separate concern of public policy. But, in this case, subsidies must be structured to reach all children in the target population. In particular, whether a child is assisted should not depend upon whether the parent chooses to work and arrange for institutional day care.

The particular application of these principles will be attempted in Chapter 5.

APPENDIX: A MODEL OF HOUSEHOLD DECISION-MAKING AND THE OPTIMAL SUBSIDY TO DAY CARE

The model developed in this appendix draws heavily on work from the author's thesis (Krashinsky, 1973) and has been inspired by the work of Lancaster (1966, 1966a) and Becker (1965). Both Lancaster and Becker suggest that important production occurs within the household. Lancaster argues that consumers combine in 'activities' goods that they purchase in order to produce 'characteristics' valued by the consumer. Shifts in the prices of goods affect not only the bundle of characteristics produced by the consumer, but also the way in which the goods are combined to produce these characteristics.

Becker emphasizes in the activities, the use of time not committed to the labour market. Thus, households combine 'time and market goods to produce more basic commodities that directly enter their utility functions' (Becker, 1965, 495).

Two basic commodities enter the household utility function in the model used here. One is child care, designated C, the other is adult consumption, designated A. Each is produced using the non-market time of the adults in the household and the goods purchased in the marketplace, where the adults exchange their time for dollars to buy the goods. For mathematical convenience, we omit the joint production of child care and household services from the model. However, C may be seen as encompassing both. Call T_A and T_C the time used directly to produce A and C respectively, and X_A and X_C the market goods used to produce A and C respectively (goods in each category are aggregated). Then, if U is the household's utility function, the process may be described by

$$A = f(X_A, T_A),\tag{1}$$

$$C = g(X_C, T_C),\tag{2}$$

$$U = U(A, C).\tag{3}$$

The parents may substitute between time and goods in producing either child care or adult consumption. In child care, for example, parents may choose to use much time and purchase only goods like food, clothing, furniture, etc., for the child. To reduce the time spent, parents may purchase goods like babysitting or day care in the marketplace. Although day care is highly labour intensive, it employs labour from outside the household. Thus from the point of view of the household, day care is a 'good.'

The household will seek to maximize $U(A, C)$ subject to the budget constraint

$$P_{XC}X_C + P_{XA}X_A = P_T(T - T_A - T_C) + S,\tag{4}$$

where P_{XC} and P_{XA} are the prices paid by the household per unit of X_C and X_A respectively, P_T is the wage received per hour of time sold in the labour market, T is the total time available, and S is all other income (including government subsidy and any non-wage income). Assume that X_A, X_C, T_A, T_C, and $T - T_A - T_C$ are all non-negative and that P_T is independent of the number of hours worked. This last assumption assumes away one imperfection in the labour market: the difficulty in finding part time work at a wage comparable to that for full time work. The price P_T can still be quite low (or zero) if the worker cannot find a reasonable job. However, since there are usually two workers in a family, requiring one wage rate poses a problem. So long as the second parent works at all (so that there is an internal maximum), P_T should be the second parent's wage rate, where by second parent one means the parent who is the primary provider of child care in the home.

This report is interested in changes in family behaviour when subsidies and taxes are introduced into the model (in particular, a subsidy to day care will reduce P_{XC}). In general the changes may be divided analytically in two: a shift in the proportions of C and A consumed, and a shift in the input ratios of time-to-goods used to produce each commodity. To emphasize this division, a simplifying assumption is introduced. Both functions A and C are assumed to be linear homogeneous. In fact, the assumption of homogeneity is all that is needed for the analytical division discussed above. The assumption of degree one (*linear homogeneity*) is mathematically convenient, but does not limit the model in any way: since A and C are measured in rather arbitrary units and affect the consumer only *through* U, any change in degree may be completely defused by a change in the structure of the utility function.

The household production functions may now be written as:

$$f(X_A, T_A) = Af(x_a, t_a),$$ (5)

$$g(X_C, T_C) = Cg(x_c, t_c),$$ (6)

where

$$x_a = \frac{X_A}{A}, x_c = \frac{X_C}{C}, t_a = \frac{T_A}{A}, \text{ and } t_c = \frac{T_C}{C},$$

and of course then

$$f(x_a, t_a) = 1,$$ (7)

$$g(x_c, t_c) = 1.$$ (8)

Given factor prices, the determination of x_c, x_a, t_c, and t_a will be independent of the amounts of C and A consumed.

To see this, note that the household is maximizing utility in equation (3), subject to the constraints in equations (4), (7), and (8). This is equivalent to maximizing the expression for L in equation (9):

$$L = U[Af(x_a, t_a), Cg(x_c, t_c)] + \alpha[1 - f(x_a, t_a)] + \beta[1 - g(x_c, t_c)]$$

$$+ \lambda[P_T T + S - (P_{XC} x_c + P_T t_c)C - (P_{XA} x_a + P_T t_a)A],$$ (9)

where α, β, and λ are Lagrangian multipliers. The conditions for maximization are expressed in equations (10) through (15) together with the constraints (4), (7), and (8).

$$\frac{\partial L}{\partial x_a} = \frac{\partial U}{\partial A} A \frac{\partial f}{\partial x_a} - \alpha \frac{\partial f}{\partial x_a} - \lambda P_{XA} A = 0,$$ (10)

$$\frac{\partial L}{\partial t_a} = \frac{\partial U}{\partial A} A \frac{\partial f}{\partial t_a} - \alpha \frac{\partial f}{\partial t_a} - \lambda P_T A = 0,$$ (11)

$$\frac{\partial L}{\partial x_c} = \frac{\partial U}{\partial C} C \frac{\partial g}{\partial x_c} - \beta \frac{\partial g}{\partial x_c} - \lambda P_{XC} C = 0, \tag{12}$$

$$\frac{\partial L}{\partial t_c} = \frac{\partial U}{\partial C} C \frac{\partial g}{\partial t_c} - \beta \frac{\partial g}{\partial t_c} - \lambda P_T C = 0, \tag{13}$$

$$\frac{\partial L}{\partial A} = \frac{\partial U}{\partial A} f - \lambda (P_{XA} x_a + P_T t_a) = 0, \tag{14}$$

$$\frac{\partial L}{\partial C} = \frac{\partial U}{\partial C} g - \lambda (P_{XC} x_c + P_T t_c) = 0. \tag{15}$$

By eliminating $\propto$, β, and λ, the constraints may be rearranged to show the independence of the goods and time ratios from the final levels of A and C. First combining equations (10) and (11), one can derive

$$\frac{\partial f / \partial x_a}{\partial f / \partial t_a} = \frac{P_{XA}}{P_T}. \tag{16}$$

This, combined with the constraint in equation (7), will solve to give x_a and t_a. Similarly equations (12) and (13) yield

$$\frac{\partial g / \partial x_c}{\partial g / \partial t_c} = \frac{P_{XC}}{P_T}, \tag{17}$$

which together with the constraint in equation (8) determine x_c and t_c. Now define P_A and P_C in equations (18) and (19).

$$P_A = P_{XA} x_a + P_T t_a, \tag{18}$$

$$P_C = P_{XC} x_c + P_T t_c. \tag{19}$$

As this problem is set up, x_a, x_c, t_a, and t_c are constants dependent on the relative prices of time and goods, so that P_A and P_C are constants independent of the relative amounts of A and C consumed. Then equations (14) and (15) yield

$$\frac{\partial U/\partial A}{\partial U/\partial C} = \frac{P_A}{P_C}, \tag{20}$$

and the constraint in equation (4) may be rewritten as

$$P_C C + P_A A = P_T T + S. \tag{21}$$

Thus P_A and P_C may be seen as the 'prices' of A and C respectively.

The maximization problem is now decomposed into two steps. The original prices P_{XA}, P_{XC}, and P_T determine x_a, t_a, x_c, t_c, and thus P_A and P_C. The derived prices P_A and P_C are now used to choose A and C so as to maximize utility.

Any sophisticated student of economics could demonstrate that in the absence of any distortions (for example, any other taxes or subsidies), a subsidy for the purchase of any particular commodity is generally economically inefficient. The subsidy is no better than, and usually much worse than a simple transfer of cash to the household in question.

Of course, the world is not void of distortions. The most relevant distortion when discussing day care is the tax on earned income. It is frequently argued that a subsidy to day care, especially for mothers on welfare, will encourage the parent to work and not only make the family better off but assist the taxpayer by reducing government expenditures. The model developed above enables one to examine how large a subsidy can be justified by this argument.

Begin by redefining the units in the production functions f and g so that one unit of X_C and one unit of X_A each cost P_X in the absence of any taxes and transfers. Now introduce a tax on earnings at the marginal rate τ_w and a subsidy at the marginal rate s_x to the purchase of X_C, the goods used in the production of child care. This defines P_{XA}, P_{XC}, and P_T as P_X, $P_X(1 - s_x)$, and $w(1 - \tau_w)$ respectively, where w is the market wage rate for the household's labour. The problem may now be defined as follows: what are the optimal values of τ_w and s_x so as to maximimize revenue for the government, keeping the family's utility at some predetermined value. An exactly equivalent problem would be to choose τ_w and s_x so as to maximize the household's utility, keeping government revenue constant. If s_x is positive, some subsidy for X_C is called for; if s_x is negative, then X_A should be subsidized.

The tax on earnings distorts the household's choice between work in the home and work in the marketplace. Under certain circumstances, it may be useful to subsidize the purchase of one of the goods at the expense of raising the general tax rate on earnings. Seen another way, τ_w taxes time when it is transformed into X_C and X_A, but not when the time is used directly in the household production function. The subsidy s_x introduces the possibility of taxing the transformation of time into X_A at a different rate than the transformation of time into X_C. This is now a problem in optimal taxation (see, for example, Diamond and Mirrlees, 1971).

The problem becomes more tractable by replacing τ_w and s_x by sales taxes τ_a and τ_c on the goods X_A and X_C respectively. The problem remains exactly equivalent if one sets

$$\tau_a = \frac{\tau_w}{1 - \tau_w}$$

and

$$\tau_c = \frac{\tau_w - s_x}{1 - \tau_w}$$

and if unearned income (S) is increased by a factor of $(1 + \tau_a)$ – the reader may check this by confirming that the budget constraint in equation (4) remains unchanged if this transformation is undertaken $(S$, of course, includes any untaxed transfer payments). The reader will note that $\tau_a = \tau_c$ implies no subsidy to either good combined with a proportional tax on earnings, while $\tau_a > \tau_c$ implies a positive subsidy to X_C combined with a tax on earnings. $\tau_c = 0$ implies that X_C ought to be subsidized at exactly the same rate as the tax on earned income. This last case might be set up by eliminating any direct subsidy, but making expenditures on X_C fully deductible from earned income before any tax is collected. It will be argued that this is the maximum subsidy to X_C justified under this model.

The problem may now be reset in terms of τ_a and τ_c as described above. This is done by redefining the prices, using the sales taxes, as

$$P_{XC} = P_X(1 + \tau_c), \tag{22}$$

$$P_{XA} = P_X(1 + \tau_a), \tag{23}$$

$$P_T = w, \tag{24}$$

and the budget constraint may be written as

$$[P_X(1 + \tau_c)x_c + wt_c]C + [P_X(1 + \tau_a)x_a + wt_a]A = wT + S. \tag{25}$$

Assume that S' is the constant transfer from the government to the family. Then the government revenue from the family, R, is

$$R = P_X \tau_c x_c C + P_X \tau_a x_a A - S'. \tag{26}$$

Given the prices in equations (22), (23), and (24), the household will choose t_a, x_a, t_c, x_c, A, and C so as to maximize utility. Given the constraint that this maximized utility should not fall below some predetermined $\bar{U}$, the problem now becomes choosing τ_a and τ_c so as to maximize R.

A pair (τ_a, τ_c) maximizes R if any change in taxes that keeps the household at the same level of utility cannot increase R. The first order condition for that constrained maximum may be stated verbally as follows: a pair (τ_a, τ_c) maximizes R if a change in τ_c (τ_a adjusted to keep utility constant) does not increase R, or

$$\left. \frac{\partial R}{\partial \tau_c} \right|_{U = \bar{U}} = 0. \tag{27}$$

Now, since $dP_T = dw = 0$, it can be shown from equations (18), (23), and (24) that

$$dP_A = P_X(1 + \tau_a)dx_a + wdt_a + P_X x_a d\tau_a. \tag{28}$$

By totally differentiating the function f, and applying equation (16), one finds that

$$P_X(1 + \tau_a)dx_a + wdt_a = 0. \tag{29}$$

Therefore

$$dP_A = P_X x_a d\tau_a. \tag{30}$$

Similarly

$$P_X(1 + \tau_c)dx_c + wdt_c = 0, \tag{31}$$

$$dP_C = P_X x_c d\tau_c. \tag{32}$$

Total differentiating the equation $U = \bar{U}$, one finds

$$\frac{\partial U}{\partial A}dA + \frac{\partial U}{\partial C}dC = 0. \tag{33}$$

From equations (20) and (33) can be derived

$$P_A dA + P_C dC = 0. \tag{34}$$

Finally, totally differentiating equation (21) yields

$$P_C dC + P_A dA + CdP_C + AdP_A = 0. \tag{35}$$

Substituting equations (30), (32), and (34) into equation (35) and solving, generates

$$d\tau_a = -\frac{x_c C}{x_a A}d\tau_c. \tag{36}$$

These changes in τ_a and τ_c will leave utility unchanged, but will change t_a, t_c, x_a, x_c, A, and C, all of which changes are required to solve equation (27). Begin by defining ϵ_a and ϵ_c as the elasticities of substitution of goods for time in the production functions f and g respectively, given the shift in relative factor prices.

$$\epsilon_a = -\frac{d(\ln x_a/t_a)}{d(\ln P_{XA}/P_T)}, \tag{37}$$

$$\epsilon_c = -\frac{d(\ln x_c/t_c)}{d(\ln P_{XC}/P_T)}. \tag{38}$$

From (22), (23), and (24) one finds

$$d(\ln P_{XA}/P_T) = \frac{d\tau_a}{1 + \tau_a}, \tag{39}$$

$$d(\ln P_{XC}/P_T) = \frac{d\tau_c}{1 + \tau_c}. \tag{40}$$

Combining equations (37), (39), and (29) yields

$$\frac{dx_a}{x_a} = -\epsilon_a \frac{d\tau_a}{1 + \tau_a} \frac{wt_a}{P_A},$$

(41)

$$\frac{dt_a}{t_a} = \epsilon_a \frac{d\tau_a}{1 + \tau_a} \frac{P_X(1 + \tau_a)x_a}{P_A}.$$

(42)

Similarly, equations (38), (40), and (31) yield

$$\frac{dx_c}{x_c} = -\epsilon_c \frac{d\tau_c}{1 + \tau_c} \frac{wt_c}{P_C},$$

(43)

$$\frac{dt_c}{t_c} = \epsilon_c \frac{d\tau_c}{1 + \tau_c} \frac{P_X(1 + \tau_c)x_c}{P_C}.$$

(44)

Now define ϵ_s as the elasticity of substitution of commodity C for commodity A given a change in the relative commodity prices (utility held constant).

$$\epsilon_s = -\frac{d(\ln C/A)}{d(\ln P_C/P_A)} \bigg|_{U=U}.$$

(45)

Substituting equations (30), (32), and (34) into equation (45), and applying the relationship between $d\tau_a$ and $d\tau_c$ in equation (36), one obtains

$$dC = -\epsilon_s \frac{P_X x_c d\tau_c C}{P_C},$$

(46)

$$dA = \epsilon_s \frac{P_X x_c d\tau_c C}{P_A}.$$

(47)

Totally differentiating equation (26), generates

$$dR = P_X[\tau_c x_c dC + \tau_c C dx_c + x_c C d\tau_c + \tau_a x_a dA + \tau_c A dx_a + x_a A d\tau_a].$$

(48)

Finally, substituting equations (36), (41), (43), (46), and (47) into equation (48) and solving yields

$$\left.\frac{dR}{d\tau_c}\right|_{U=\bar{U}} = P_X x_c C \left[\frac{\tau_a}{1+\tau_a} \frac{\epsilon_s P_X (1+\tau_a)x_a + \epsilon_a wt_a}{P_A} \right.$$

$$\left. - \frac{\tau_c}{1+\tau_c} \frac{\epsilon_s P_X (1+\tau_c)x_c + \epsilon_c wt_c}{P_C} \right]. \tag{49}$$

Equation (36) indicates that to keep utility constant, $d\tau_c$ and $d\tau_a$ have different signs, so that as τ_c rises, τ_a must fall. At $\tau_c = 0$, clearly $(dR/d\tau_c)_{U=\bar{U}}$ is greater than zero, so that τ_c should be raised. Symmetrically, if τ_c is raised until $\tau_a = 0$, then $(dR/d\tau_c)_{U=\bar{U}}$ is less than zero and τ_c should be lowered. The desired maximum revenue occurs where both τ_a and τ_c exceed zero.

Returning to the (τ_w, s_x) notation, this implies that τ_w, the tax on earned income is positive (since $\tau_w = \tau_a / [1 + \tau_a]$) while s_x, the subsidy to child care, is less than τ_w ($s_x = [\tau_a - \tau_c]/[1+\tau_a]$). To obtain the sign of s_x, we set $\tau_a = \tau_c = \tau_0$ and examine the sign of $(dR/d\tau_c)_{U=U}$. If the sign is negative, then τ_c should be lowered and τ_a raised to maximize revenue, and s_x, the subsidy to child care should be positive. With $\tau_a = \tau_c = \tau_0$ in equation (49), one obtains

$$\left.\frac{dR}{d\tau_c}\right|_{U=\bar{U}} = P_X x_c C \frac{\tau_0}{1+\tau_0} \left[\frac{\epsilon_s P_X (1+\tau_0)x_a + \epsilon_a wt_a}{P_A} \right.$$

$$\left. - \frac{\epsilon_s P_X (1+\tau_0)x_c + \epsilon_c wt_c}{P_C} \right]. \tag{50}$$

Equation (50) may be rewritten in a more useful manner by subtracting from the bracketed expression on the right-hand side of equation (50) the following expression which is equal to zero

$$\frac{\epsilon_s P_X (1+\tau_0)x_a + \epsilon_s wt_a}{P_A} - \frac{\epsilon_s P_X (1+\tau_0)x_c + \epsilon_s wt_c}{P_C} \tag{51}$$

$$\left[= \frac{\epsilon_s P_A}{P_A} - \frac{\epsilon_s P_C}{P_C} = 0 \right].$$

This will transform equation (50) into:

$$\frac{dR}{d\tau_c}\bigg|_{U=\bar{U}} = P_X x_c C \frac{\tau_0}{1+\tau_0}\left[\frac{(\epsilon_a - \epsilon_s)wt_a}{P_A} - \frac{(\epsilon_c - \epsilon_s)wt_c}{P_C}\right].$$ (52)

Thus the sign of $(dr\,/\,d\tau_c)\bigg|_{U=\bar{U}}$

depends upon the relative sizes of the elasticities ϵ_a, ϵ_c and ϵ_s and the relative 'time-intensiveness' of the commodities A and C (since wt_a/P_A and wt_c/P_C represent the fraction of the total price of A and C respectively that goes towards the 'purchase' of time).

To argue that child care should be subsidized, it is sufficient to argue that ϵ_c is larger than ϵ_a and that child care is more time-intensive than other adult commodities. This is not unreasonable. In taking care of children, parents have considerable access to goods in the marketplace (babysitting, day care). Small changes in circumstances and relative prices have induced many households in recent years to make outside arrangements for child care, freeing up to fifty hours each week to seek market employment. Alternatively, parents leaving the labour force can save significant amounts formerly spent on goods by reassuming the care of the children.

It is much less easy for adults to substitute time and goods in the rest of their consumption. One can buy pre-cooked dinners, or eat in restaurants, or hire a gardener to save time, but the limits on this process are more rigid than for child care. Leisure goods, a large component of A, require time for consumption in fairly rigid proportions. Is it possible to save time by purchasing extra goods in consuming a concert or a play or a vacation abroad?

The large amount of time spent with children, even when day care is employed, might also suggest the greater time intensity of the commodity child care. Technically, one need only assume equal time intensities for A and C, so long as $\epsilon_c > \epsilon_a$, to ensure a subsidy to child care.

If a subsidy to child care is justified, how large should it be? It has been seen that s_x (the subsidy rate to day care) never exceeds τ_w (the tax rate on wages). But s_x will approach τ_w if $\tau_a \gg \tau_c$ (where $\gg$ signifies the relationship 'much greater than'). From equation (49), this will occur only if

$$\frac{\epsilon_s P_X(1 + \tau_c)x_c + \epsilon_c wt_c}{P_C} \gg \frac{\epsilon_s P_X(1 + \tau_a)x_a + \epsilon_a wt_a}{P_A}.$$ (53)

And equation (53) can hold only if $\epsilon_c \gg \epsilon_a$ *and* either if ϵ_s is very small (relative to ϵ_c) or if A is very time intensive, so that the term on the right-hand side of (53), $\epsilon_s P_X (1 + \tau_a) x_a / P_A$, is insignificant. It has already been suggested that ϵ_c might be large relative to ϵ_a. It is also possible to argue that ϵ_s is very small. Most parents might be assumed to resist strongly a reduction in their children's consumption and welfare even when relative prices (P_C and P_A) shift, although knowing relative prices in advance may affect the number of children parents desire. One might assume that parents seek to provide C and A (roughly, consumption for their children and direct consumption for themselves) in some more or less fixed proportion, whatever the relative prices. This would make ϵ_s close to zero.

In fact, some empirical work seems to bear this out. It has been shown (Leibowitz, 1974, S113) that more highly educated parents spend more time with their children than do less educated parents. Since more highly educated parents tend to have higher wage rates, this would suggest in the model that t_c is lower and P_C / P_A is higher (if C is time-intensive relative to A) for these parents. These parents would only spend more time with their children if C were significantly higher among wealthier parents (than among poorer parents), suggesting that the ϵ_s is quite small.

It should be noted that a large ϵ_c and a small ϵ_s are not contradictory. Parents may alter the ways in which C is produced wthout lowering the level of C.

If $\tau_c \approx 0$, so that $s_x \approx \tau_w$, then this is equivalent either to making expenditures on X_C fully deductible from wage income before that income is taxed, or to subsidizing X_C at a rate no greater than the marginal tax rate. Thus the maximum subsidy for children's goods that can be justified by the efficiency arguments of this model amounts to income tax deductibility for expenditures on children's goods.

This is not an argument for tax deductibility of child care as a work expense. Work takes time away from child care, but work also takes time away from all other activities. Rather tax deductibility rests on the particularly high elasticity of substitution of goods for time in producing child care, and the particularly low elasticity of substitution of child care for other commodities in consumption.

Of course, an argument for partial deductibility could also be applied to other commodities like laundry and housekeeping with high goods-for-time elasticities of substitution. But child care is a special commodity. The approximation $\tau_c = 0$ (full deductibility) makes it simple to administer, and the high cost of child care makes deductibility an important issue both for efficiency and for equity.

While the optimization problem maximized revenue, leaving utility constant, the same results are obtained by maximizing utility, subject to constant revenue.

In the latter case, deductibility of child care purchases might generate revenue, if enough parents were induced to expand their participation in the labour force, and if they could be absorbed into the labour market. Such a change could have the desirable characteristic of providing a deduction and allowing for a decrease in overall tax rates.

5

Present policies towards day care subsidies in Ontario: evaluation and a proposal

INTRODUCTION

At times in the past, day care subsidies have been seen by many as a form of welfare assistance to families who were unable for some reason to provide 'normal' care for their children. For mothers who were disabled, or suffering from mental illness or alcoholism, day care could help preserve the family until the problem was overcome. This view of day care could also be extended to justify subsidies to help single-parent families where work by the parent in the labour force might keep the family off welfare. Pushing the argument even further, day care subsidies are now offered to two-parent families in which the mother's income is needed to maintain a reasonable standard of living.

This report has no quarrel with fully subsidized day care for families with special needs. Where day care is being used not to free the mother for work but to relieve an intolerable situation, there can be little value in replacing a day care subsidy with a reduced tax rate on earnings (as discussed in Chapter 4). Although economic theory might argue that a cash transfer is superior to a transfer 'in kind,' that theory assumes that consumers are entirely rational. When a family is unable to make rational decisions, there is a role for some public intervention. But to extend this reasoning in order to provide free day care to perfectly competent parents contemplating labour market participation is to promote inefficiency.

Public policy has been slow to come to grips with the phenomenon of working mothers. The labour force participation rates cited in Chapter 2 suggest that a mother's entry into the labour force is not an aberration. Two out of every five mothers work; one out of three mothers with preschool children works. Day care policy must reflect this reality. At a time when day care subsidies are being used increasingly to assist women in the labour force, it is wise to question whether this represents the best use of scarce public funds.

In this chapter, the current policies towards day care are analysed, with particular attention to how these policies conform with the optimal policies developed in Chapter 4. Some new directions for day care development are suggested and some attention is paid to how different levels of public funding might be applied most effectively.

The chapter begins by describing how day care subsidies are currently administered in Ontario. Policy regarding single-parent and two-parent families is examined, and these policies are evaluated in terms of the criteria developed in Chapter 4. The experience in other parts of Canada and other countries towards day care is considered in order to assist in understanding the debate now in progress in Ontario. Ways in which day care subsidies might be improved are suggested. Special attention is paid to separating out issues of redistribution from those of efficiency. A proposal is offered to show how public policy might attempt to reach children in need. The cost of some of the proposals and how the benefits would be distributed are discussed. The possible impact of day care subsidies on labour force participation and on fertility is analysed. Finally, some of the policy implications of the discussion in this chapter are summarized.

SUBSIDIES TO DAY CARE IN ONTARIO IN 1976

In general, Ontario subsidizes day care under the guidelines of the Canada Assistance Plan, as discussed earlier. Families qualify for day care subsidies on the basis of need when no parent is available to care for the children. In computing the day care subsidy, 'needs' are calculated by adding expenditures on food, clothing, personal items, utilities, housing, taxes, work-related expenses (travel), and medical needs. The first three, being hard to document, are taken from a table, while actual expenses are taken for the other items. Then net income is computed by taking total earned income and exempting 25 per cent. The difference between net income and needs is, if it is positive, the day care fee charged to the parent. The remainder of the full cost of day care is subsidized.

There is some room for discretion in assessing needs; for example, Toronto has a rather generous exemption for contingencies. While a detailed critique of needs testing is beyond the intent of this report, some obvious problems emerge. As family income rises (or even if it does not rise), families have every incentive to upgrade their housing rather than pay more for day care, since 'actual' rent or mortgage payments are the basis for need in the family budget. Additional rent or mortgage payments are subsidized 100 per cent by the government through a reduction in the day care fee, although one might argue that one's mortgage payment would depend on when the home was purchased, and that those unlucky enough to have bought a home after prices rose do require more assistance. Similarly, families who have incurred large consumer debts receive higher day care subsidies. Aside from questions about the structuring of incentives, the reliance on the interpretation of the welfare administrator may add to the arbitrariness and administrative expense in the system.

When day care subsidies are warranted, they are paid only for the use of full-day day care in either a municipal day care centre or a private centre which has negotiated a purchase of service agreement with the municipality. This creates the inefficiencies discussed in Chapter 4. Parents are induced to use the most expensive kind of day care when reliable care may well be available at far less cost from relatives or neighbours. Parents are induced to work even when that decision is not economically efficient were the parent to be faced with the true cost of care and with the full market wage.

It is useful to divide our analysis into two parts at this point. Single-parent families (and two-parent families in which one parent is incapacitated) face a somewhat different system than do two-parent families. A single-parent family may well qualify for both welfare and a day care subsidy, so that the total system of benefits must be examined. The two-parent family is off welfare once one parent works full time, so that only day care subsidies need be considered.

(a) Single-parent families

Single-parent families qualify for Family Benefits, a provincial program for particular groups of poor people that includes the disabled and the blind as well. Family Benefits is a somewhat more generous plan than General Welfare Assistance, a municipally run program to fund on a short-term basis the needs of all families without a member employed full time, so that the single-parent family generally chooses to come under Family Benefits. The Family Benefits program assesses 'need' much as does the day care program, except that a table is used for housing costs, and net income exempts 25 per cent of earned income *plus* $100 per month. The difference between need and net income is the Family Benefits Allowance.

In 1975, a family consisting of a mother and two children would qualify for a Family Benefits Allowance of $3936 if the mother earned no income. In addition, the family would be eligible for subsidized rent in Ontario Housing (if the family could get in), subsidized OHIP premiums, family allowance, and an Ontario tax credit. The Ontario Economic Council estimates the value of these additional benefits at $2678, and has prepared a table which summarizes the changes in the various programs as earned income rises (Ontario Economic

Council, 1976, 26). Assuming that the family uses $2000 worth of day care and neglecting the current minimum charge of 25¢ per day, that table is presented in somewhat altered form as Table 21. (See Appendix for Table 21 and the other tables in this chapter.)

Because the family loses Family Benefits when the mother works full time, single parents will have little incentive to do so unless their wage rate is high. This sudden fall off in benefits when the work week exceeds thirty hours is called a 'notch,' and it is clearly an irrational policy. Even with free day care, a parent earning $5000 per year in full-time work will see the family's income rise by only $600. The family may gain even less if it is fortunate enough to live in a municipality with a number of geared-to-income programs (programs that are withdrawn as earned income rises) in which the family participates. Such programs include the subsidizing of visiting homemakers, drugs, consumer durables, recreation (summer camps, etc.), adult education, and job skills upgrading, etc.

The notch makes it somewhat difficult to see clearly the impact of day care subsidies in the neighbourhood of the notch. Suppose now that the notch is eliminated so that the Family Benefits are paid so long as the family meets the needs test. Assume a basic allowance of $6500 to this family (incorporate rent and OHIP subsidies and the family allowance into the basic 'guarantee' when the parent does not work) and a tax back rate of 75 per cent over an income exemption of $1200. Day care, costing $2000, is provided at no charge to the family as long as Family Benefits are received. When the benefits run out (that is, fall to $800, since family allowances and tax credits do not disappear as income rises), families begin paying towards day care 75¢ of each additional dollar earned. *Other* than the 'notch,' this is not an unrealistic picture of the current welfare system.

It was determined in Chapter 4 that the 'optimal day care subsidy' to help the family should not exceed deductibility. The notchless system designed above is compared in Table 22 with a system in which the family pays for its own day care, but is allowed to deduct that payment before computing benefits and/or taxes. With deductibility, the income exemption is raised to $1867 so that the two systems will be comparable and will rejoin the positive income tax table at the same point. It may be seen that the final positions for the family are identical, *except* at low earned incomes, where the needs test approach to day care fees is more favourable to the family's 'total income after day care charge.'

To see why the needs test is inefficient, observe that the parent contemplating part-time work for ten weeks per year at the minimum wage of $2.40 will earn $840 while using day care costing $400. For an efficient decision, the net money gain of $440 should be weighed against the additional cost of working (lost productivity in the home, work related expenses), taking into account any future gains in income discussed earlier, and any psychic benefits from working (pride in self-sufficiency, fellowship in the working place, etc.). But in Table 22, free day care makes the net money gain not $440 but $840, distorting the decision.

This problem can be seen more clearly in Table 23 which compares deductibility and the needs test for a single parent with two preschool children, assuming day care costs in the Metro day care centre of $2400 per child (not unrealistic in 1975). If this parent considers working full time at $2.40 per hour, then the annual earnings of $4200 (assume a fifty-week year) must be weighed against day care costs of $4800. The net loss in the marketplace is $600 ($4800 worth of resources are used to free the time of the parent, who produces $4200 in value in the work place), which must be weighed against the negative and positive factors in working discussed above. This decision is preserved under deductibility (Scheme B in the table), but the needs test *increases* the family's income (after day care) by $1950 when this parent works. Clearly, work by this parent might well be inefficient, yet it is encouraged by the needs test. The cost is borne by the government, which pays the parent $6500 to stay home, but incurs total expenditures of $9050 when the parent works full time ($4800 in day care costs plus $4250 in benefits). The argument may be carried even further by increasing the number of children and by adding infants, as was done in Chapter 4.

(b) *Two-parent families*

The two-parent family in which one parent is already working does not qualify for welfare assistance. However, under the 'needs' test, the family may still qualify for day care subsidy. Since 'needs' includes the actual rent (or mortgage payments and property taxes), as well as some debt payments for families in difficulty, the monthly budget for a family may be quite large – possibly over $700 for a family of five. If the budget exceeds earnings minus exemptions, then the fee for day care is zero. Otherwise, net earnings minus the budget comprise the fee.[1]

Many families will be eligible to receive complete subsidy under the needs test. To see this, note that 25 per cent of earnings are exempted, and that further exemptions of $750 might well be allowed for 'contingencies.' Assume a budget for needs of $8500 for a family of five. This budget is high but not extraordinary, given the cost of rents or mortgage payments in Toronto in 1975.

---

1 The fee for day care is computed using 'Form 7, The Day Nurseries Act, Determination of Available Income,' a form supplied by the Ministry of Community and Social Services.

In this case the family will receive the full subsidy for day care as long as family income is less than $12,333 *after tax*. With one preschool child in day care, *net* family earnings (after tax income, not including the family allowance) must reach $16,000 before all the day care subsidy disappears. Roughly this would correspond to before tax earnings of almost $20,000. With two preschoolers, there will be some subsidy until before-tax earnings reach $24,000. This situation is laid out in some detail in Table 24.

The 'optimal subsidy' to help the family was shown to be a maximum of deductibility. While the income tax rate on the earnings of a second parent is significant, it hardly justifies the full subsidies received by some families. Since the primary income earner loses the marital exemption as the second parent begins to work, essentially there is no personal exemption for the second parent. For approximately the first $2000 earned by the second parent, the family's taxes rise at the top marginal rate of the first parent. At that point, any further earnings are taxed directly under the federal and provincial income tax. For example, if a wife earns $6000, and the husband's top marginal rate is 27 per cent, then the family income taxes will rise by approximately $1100 ($444 due to the husband's loss of the married exemption, and about $650 paid directly by the wife; see Revenue Canada, 1975).

The rate of subsidy to day care should optimally be no more than 20-25 per cent for most families. Yet that subsidy can, in fact, run from zero up to 100 per cent. The point *is not* that it would be efficient simply to eliminate day care subsidies. The point *is* that much of the day care subsidy should be replaced by a reduction in the tax rate on the second parent's earnings.

Tax law seems to reflect the view that women work for money to purchase luxuries, so that their earnings ought to be taxed at a rate well above that faced by the family's first wage earner. Certainly this is not true for most families in which both parents work. And in a family with young children, the entry into the labour force of the second parent imposes significant costs on the family. These costs include not only child care, but the loss of the time used for cooking, cleaning, shopping, and the numerous other tasks important in running a household. The gain to the family when the second parent works is far less than the gain when the first parent enters the labour force, yet taxes are much higher on the second parent. Small wonder than an American study found that women were unwilling to pay for child care of their choice much more than 30 per cent of their gross earnings (Rowe, 1971).

One might argue that the full subsidy to day care afforded some families is an attempt to compensate for this high tax rate. Two difficulties make this policy highly inefficient: the subsidy is now distirbuted unevenly, and even if it were more generally available, it would lead to a poor use of public funds.

First, consider who may receive the subsidy. In Metro Toronto, not all two-parent families are aware of the possibilities for subsidy, and of those that are aware, not all can enter the program. Toronto day care funds are limited and rationed on the basis of priority (with single-parent and multi-problem families naturally at the top of the list), so that many families technically eligible for subsidy do not receive it.[2]

Also, as was pointed out earlier, subsidies apply only in municipal day care or in private day care centres that have concluded agreements with the municipality. Many parents who would be eligible for partial subsidy do not wish to pay the high fees in the formal centres and so make alternate arrangements (for which no subsidy is available). In Ottawa, where there are no waiting lists for subsidy, and where fees in municipal centres have been raised only recently to reflect full costs, there is some evidence to suggest that parents are reluctant to use formal day care when the charge gets too close to full cost (when subsidies become too partial). Peel reports a similar reluctance by parents to pay much beyond the $5 per day charge that had been the maximum fee before fees were raised to retain eligibility for federal funds.[3]

This gives rise to the interesting hypothesis, frequently advanced as fact, that only the very rich and the very poor can afford to use day care centres. General observations would bear this out: in Metro Toronto centres few parents receive partial subsidy, implying that those with middle-range incomes tend to avoid day care centres.

The predominance of children receiving full subsidy in public centres gives rise to the problem, discussed earlier, of centres that contain only children from poor (generally single-parent) and multi-problem homes. This imposes additional costs on municipal centres. Perhaps more importantly, the homogeneity of the public centres seriously limits the variety of experiences available to disadvantaged children, making it more difficult for them to avoid falling behind their more affluent counterparts.

Secondly, full day care subsidies are subject to the same inefficiencies discussed earlier – they induce work for women who, by standards of economic efficiency, should remain out of the labour force for several years. This applies chiefly to the lower income women who now are the ones who do qualify for full subsidy. Consider Table 24. In a family in which the husband earns $8000 net, a job for the wife at $4000 net (which in 1975 was above the minimum wage), when child care costs $4800, is justified only if the psychic and other net benefits from working (including the negative benefit of lost home productivity) compensate for the $800 loss in income. But the day care subsidy removes

2 Conversation with officials at Metropolitan Toronto Department of Social Services.
3 Conversation with the Commissioners of Social Services in both regions.

$4800 in costs from the family, making the job in the market appear to the family to generate a gain in output of $4000. This makes work quite attractive, whereas economic efficiency would dictate otherwise.

It should be noted that aside from any provincial subsidy, child care expenditures by the working parent are tax deductible, within severe limits, in computing federal and provincial income taxes. When both parents worked in 1975, a maximum of $500 per child in child care expenses might be deducted (up to a maximum of $2000 for four children). The limit was raised in 1976 to $1000 per child (up to $4000 for four children). Since, even in lower-cost private centres in Toronto, care for preschoolers cost at least $1800 per year in 1975, the limit is still too low.

In addition, the need for the claimants of the deduction to provide receipts has been complicated by the fact that many informal care-givers will deal only in cash. The present low value of the deduction may result in many parents being unwilling to jeopardize their care arrangements by requesting receipts, thus losing out entirely on the tax advantage.

THE EXPERIENCE ELSEWHERE

(a) *Other provinces in Canada*

Ontario could benefit from the experiences with day care in some other parts of Canada, particularly British Columbia. In Canada, all provinces subsidize day care under the cost sharing agreements of the Canada Assistance Plan (CAP), and most employ a needs test similar to that of Ontario. British Columbia has employed a means test, in which the parents' contribution to day care is related to both family income and family size, but not to any assessment of needs; the point where the family begins to contribute to day care is not related to the individual family's budget – rent, debts, food, special diets or medication, etc. (Province of British Columbia, 1974). The means test allows a tax back rate of 50 per cent, instead of the minimum of 75 per cent for the needs test under CAP. Unfortunately, the high cost of housing in British Columbia urban areas particularly affects young families (the kind that use day care). Howard Clifford, day care consultant to CAP, commented that the province has had to retreat to using the needs test for the majority of those families receiving subsidy.[4]

The B.C. program was liberal enough to subsidize 12,950 children, of whom over 10,000 were 5 years old or younger, with total expenditures in 1974 of $10,198,000 (Province of British Columbia, 1974, 30-6). In contrast, Ontario

---

4 Interview in Ottawa, 25 November 1975, with Howard Clifford, Day Care Consultant to the Canada Assistance Plan.

supported 13,075 children in day care with expenditures of $11.7 million (see Chapter 2). However, the 1971 Census shows Ontario with more than three and a half times as many children as British Columbia, 781,000 against 213,000 (Hepworth, 1975, 62 and 75). The reasons for higher per capita expenditures in B.C. do not include the quality of care. The province limited the cost of day care subsidized to $120 per month, and required that centres serving any subsidized child could not charge more than $120 per month to unsubsidized children. This is well below the cost of care in Ontario. However, British Columbia subsidies are granted through a 'coupon' given to parents that can be cashed by any care giver. The province subsidizes not only day care centres and family day care (4190 and 3071 spaces respectively in 1974), but also paid care in the child's own home – 2022 spaces in 1974 (Province of British Columbia, 1974, 31). The maximum charge in the child's own home and in Family day care is $90 per month (British Columbia, 1975, especially 18-21).

The British Columbia sliding fee scale does involve the inefficiency discussed earlier of inducing into the labour force those for whom work might be inefficient. However, British Columbia avoids somewhat the incentives in Ontario for subsidized parents to use day care centres over informal, reliable, cheaper modes of care (neighbours, relatives, etc.). The Province of British Columbia will still pay part of the charge for in-home child care for these parents. However, since the sliding scale fixes the contribution of parents who are subsidized, parents are not *discouraged* from using the more expensive day care centres over less expensive babysitting.

No other province runs as elaborate a program as British Columbia. Most accept the CAP guidelines. Manitoba, however, is resisting the CAP regulation that only parents in need can be subsidized. Manitoba requires that no centre serving subsidized children charge more than $5 per diem to any child in the centre. Of course, our earlier cost figures suggest that $5 per diems are impossible unless staff-child ratios are well below one to eight, the number recommended by the Manitoba day care program's field staff.[5] Therefore Manitoba pays a flat subsidy to the centres for each child served (whether or not that child would qualify for subsidy under CAP). CAP shares in the cost of this additional subsidy only for those children who qualify under CAP guidelines. This compromise would make one optimistic that other innovations in day care finance might also benefit from some cost-sharing under CAP.

5 Data are contained in a letter from Roxy Freedman, Director, Child Day Care Program, Division of Social Security, Manitoba Department of Health and Social Development, Winnipeg, Manitoba R3G 0R4.

(b) *Other countries*

Other countries, of course, treat day care somewhat differently. Many provide day care on a sliding fee scale (geared to income), but it is common to subsidize all parents using day care by placing a ceiling on the parent's contribution. This is done in Sweden and Norway. In Norway the maximum monthly charge is $28 per child (Ekrem, 1973; Karen et al., 1973), and in the cities 12 per cent of the child population is in day care centres. In Japan, the top monthly fee is $20, but the quality of care is much lower (Takahashi, 1973). And, of course, the Eastern European countries subsidize day care heavily. Surprisingly, however, at least one Eastern European country – Hungary – has become mindful of the high cost of inducing all women to work, and has introduced a child-care grant to induce mothers to stay at home with young children (Ferge, 1973).

In the U.S., day care has been administered under a wide spectrum of programs, varying from retraining and job programs for welfare mothers ('Work Incentive Program') to high quality education programs ('Head Start'). Attempts to develop a comprehensive child care bill have been unsuccessful. The federal welfare programs have matched local funds for day care and provided day care to poor areas, although the programs are not always income tested (for a discussion of U.S. day care policy, see Young and Nelson, 1974). Many proposals for day care in recent years in the United States have been tied up with work requirements for parents on welfare, a policy generally not viewed favourably by Canada (although Canadians are very concerned with maintaining work incentives: see Lalonde, 1973).

SOME ALTERNATIVES FOR ONTARIO: A PROPOSAL

(a) *Day care to help families*

It should be clear that the debate over day care subsidies is not simply a debate over economic efficiencies. Day care subsidies serve as a wage subsidy that can reduce somewhat the very high tax rates on earned income faced by either the single parent or the second parent in the two-parent family. It has become obvious that the subsidy as presently administered in Ontario tends to be inefficient. The full subsidy encourages the entry into the labour force of women for whom work is inefficient at this particular time, and subsidies to day care bias care arrangements towards the most expensive kind of care. But eliminating day care subsidies without any other change in policy would make many families significantly worse off.

Day care is an attractive issue on which to fight for a redistribution of income. Voters who might be 'turned off' by a plea for reduced tax rates might well be more responsive to an emotional discussion of better care for children.

But if the goal is to help families, day care subsidies beyond deductibility are an inefficient way to achieve that goal. Stated another way, families would be made better off at far less cost to the government through the use of other policies.

To make rational policy, the issues of redistribution and efficiency must be resolved separately. How much income do we wish to redistribute to poor families? How much tax burden should be borne by working mothers? Once the redistributional issue is settled, the economist can propose the most efficient way to achieve that redistribution. The advocate of subsidized day care is making two separate arguments: one is that certain families are unfairly treated by current tax law (including the tax back of benefits from welfare clients); the second is that day care subsidies would be a good way to change that treatment. The first one is a political issue. The second is an economic question, and one must reply that subsidies are not efficient. But the rejection of day care subsidies as inefficient *does not* resolve the question of income redistribution. For example, for public policy to respond to a request for food from a poor family by stating that in kind transfers are inefficient and thus no aid can be provided, hardly solves the family's problem. To respond to the same request by suggesting that the family may have its own tastes, so that an in kind transfer would be inefficient, and then providing a cash grant to buy food, represents a far different outcome.

A common proposal for day care is to charge parents fees on a sliding scale with income. This is generally a variation on the needs test discussed above. The principal problem here is one of efficiency. Parents who would earn the lowest incomes would pay the lowest day care fees, yet on efficiency grounds these are the last parents who should be induced to enter the labour force and use high-cost institutional day care.[6] The low productivity of these parents in the labour force does not outweigh the high cost of day care combined with the loss of production within the household when the parent works. Yet these are the very people most affected by the subsidy. If these parents prefer to care for their own children, it may well be most effective to direct funds towards the family to allow the parent to do so. However, if the choice is between no income redistribution at all, and income redistribution by day care subsidy, one must

6 It may be argued that fees based upon an 'ability to pay' would ensure that all families had equal access to day care and thus would be more 'just' (but inefficient). Although this is a non-economic argument, the economist can only point out that it is an unusual view of justice. The problem facing the poor is a low level of 'access' to all purchased commodities. It is unclear why it is just to ensure equal access to some commodities (day care, for example) but not to others (food, clothing, transportation, vacations, etc.). The real issue would seem to be how to achieve the desired increase in the well-being of poor families at the least cost to the public purse (that is, to other taxpayers).

decide whether the inefficiency of subsidies is so high as to make redistribution unattractive.

As another example, it is frequently suggested that public funds are most urgently needed to provide infant day care. But in Metro Toronto municipal day nurseries, where one adult cares for two infants, costs of care run well over $4000 per child per year. Unless the mother is extremely productive in the labour force, this type of care must be inefficient. Imagine, for example, a low-wage mother with two infants. Can one conceivably justify spending over $8000 to free this mother to work for well under $5000 per year, especially when the day care may well represent no improvement upon the care being given the child by the mother within the home? Yet someone interested in more assistance for this family may well support infant day care if no other program is politically acceptable.

The economist *can* make the following statement. If it is decided to redistribute income towards families with young children, it is far more efficient to reduce marginal tax rates and to increase cash transfers than to provide heavily subsidized day care. This might be achieved for single-parent families on welfare by allowing them an additional exemption on earned income before welfare benefits were computed, where that exemption would be equal to the cost of institutional day care for the children in the family. The exemption would not depend upon the actual cost of day care. Even more simply, the marginal tax rate can be reduced significantly from 75 per cent and all day care expenses made deductible. In each case, parents would make the efficient decision on labour force entry (dependent on wage rate relative to actual day care costs) and would have the incentive to use the most efficient form of child care.

For two-parent families, all child care expenses should be made deductible for tax purposes. To further help these families, the high rate of taxation might be reduced. This might be achieved without confusing the tax tables by allowing a further deduction to the second parent in a family (the one with the lower income) in order to reduce net income.

It should be pointed out that replacing the current system of day care subsidies with the alternative of reduced tax (back) rates will change somewhat the relative well-being of the various families qualifying for subsidy. If the tax rate is reduced to ensure that no family now receiving subsidies is made worse off, then many families formerly eligible for subsidies but having available low cost alternative arrangements will be significantly better off. Since many families are now eligible for partial subsidy but do not take advantage of it because formal day care is still too expensive, and since these families would now benefit by reduced tax rates (assuming they have always worked and used low cost alternative care), public expenditures may well rise. Of course the lower tax rate increases work incentives, and a higher labour force participation rate would increase tax revenues. In a sense, the differential effects on various families are inevitable. If the 'correct' market signals are to be given, then those with low cost child care arrangements must be given a financial incentive to use them.

A principal difficulty in all these proposals is that they would depend not only upon Ontario but upon changes in federal taxation and in the Canada Assistance Plan (unless Ontario is to absorb the whole cost of the proposals). On the other hand, the alternative of large increases in day care subsidies would also not be shareable under CAP. The simple truth is that significant redistributions of income are almost invariably going to involve the federal government. There has been a trend in recent years for governments to take even larger portions of GNP in taxes, returning, in exchange, an ever larger number of services. Whether this trend could be reversed in day care is not clear.

(b) *Day care to help children – preschoolers*
It was made clear in Chapter 4 that additional subsidies to child care might be justified by a desire to help disadvantaged children. What is also clear is that to reach all children in the target population in an efficient manner, one might not want to direct all subsidies to full-day day care (unless it were determined that children could only be reached in all-day programs). If an enriched program were judged useful to children, such a program should reach children whether or not their parents worked. This report can suggest how such a program might be set up, although, obviously, the exact design would require detailed consultation with experts in early childhood education.

The program naturally would involve higher costs and higher staff-child ratios per hour than the current minimum day care programs in Ontario (see the earlier discussion of quality). It is also unlikely that an enriched program would be most efficient beyond a period of 2-3 hours each day. The public program would provide all parents with vouchers entitling their children to free tuition in an enriched nursery school program, along with free transportation to and from programs. When parents do not work and children are cared for in the home the voucher could be used at any nursery school offering a program approved by the public authority. The nursery school can then cash the voucher in for an amount specified in the legislation (a uniform per diem could be established for all approved schools). Private nurseries may charge parents a fee beyond the voucher. However, it is expected that public nursery schools will be established to provide a standard of programming at no additional charge beyond the voucher. One might envision staff-child ratios of one to five for children aged two to five years.

When parents work, the voucher can be used in a number of ways. When the children attend a day care centre, the voucher will cover the cost of the enriched program to be offered at some time during the day. With the high level of supervision present during the enriched program, it might be acceptable to relax staff requirements during the rest of the day. This goes along with the suggestion by some day care administrators that staff ratio requirements are too rigid and that ratios should be set according to function and program, rather than to some constant standard.[7] Thus, the parents would pay for custodial care during the rest of the day, while a high-level program was provided for two to three hours, perhaps in two segments during the day (the exact design of such a scheme is beyond an economist's competence). The combination of lower staff ratios and the shorter day (paid for by parents) could reduce day care fees substantially. Assuming a reduction in staff ratios of 20 per cent and the reduction in the custodial day by 30 per cent, costs to the parent could be reduced by almost 50 per cent. The most efficient way to enrich a day care program would, of course, involve some experimentation and variation, especially at the beginning.

When children are cared for by babysitters, either in the home of the child or the home of the sitter, the voucher could be used in a neighbourhood nursery school. By giving the sitter a substantial break during the day, fees might be expected to come down (by the normal market processes). The program will guarantee to each child whose parents work a professionally run, high-level, developmental program.

For children cared for in family day care, some middle ground can be worked out. If the day care mother supervises only one or two children, the centralized program is the obvious one. For the day care mother with five children, a program run in the mother's home by a visiting teacher is an option (perhaps too expensive an option).

The enriched program would also provide a connection to the whole range of informal care arrangements made by working parents. Since virtually all children would attend the program, those running it could become familiar with those providing care for the rest of the day. Where problems were perceived to exist, some action could be initiated – these problems might be noticed through the child itself or at the time when the child is brought to and from the program (and some contact made with the sitter).

The voucher system allows for some flexibility in dealing with different children. If it is judged that certain children are in need of more intensive

7 This represents the *author's interpretation* of some of the comments of Assistant Deputy Minister John Anderson in the Ministry of Community and Social Services in an interview with the author on 16 September 1975.

programs, those children could be given special vouchers allowing the child to attend either two sessions of the normal nursery school each day or – more likely – a special more costly program (perhaps also of longer duration than two to three hours) elsewhere. For example, it may be judged that children from particularly disadvantaged homes – extreme poverty, alcoholism in the home, or just single-parent families – require a daily five-hour enriched program to enter public school on a level with other children. These children would receive vouchers worth much more than usual to support approved special programs.

It should be clear that a scheme such as that described above meets the criteria established earlier. It does not distort the parent's decision about work in the market or in the household (or, rather, it allows the least possible distortion from the optimal result). It maintains the incentive to the parent to make whatever arrangements for care are most convenient; for example, a mother who has arranged with grandmother to care for the child has no economic incentive to use expensive full day care. The scheme reaches all children, whatever the parents' decision about child care, and we can adjust the program to meet the special needs of particular children.

It is realized that such a program would require some special arrangement with the federal government to ensure at least some cost-sharing under CAP. This problem is solvable so long as the federal government does not choose to use the opportunity to opt out entirely from the funding of day care. In the limit, the spirit of the Canada Assistance Plan would be consistent with sharing the costs for those children in families below median income (as CAP does today). And Ontario would find some willing allies in other provinces for its demands.

(c) Day care for school children

The treatment of school age children is, of course, a different matter entirely. After a full day of school, child care as 'transfers to children' hardly seem justifiable. However, it is in this area that real innovation is possible. As we have seen, child care for school age children is almost as expensive as preschool care. In large part this is because of the time split. Care is needed before school, during lunch, and after school, and staffing three separate times is expensive. In many parts of the U.S, children naturally eat their lunches in school, a practice that allows the federal government to subsidize the provision of nutritious hot meals for the students. Given a desire to transfer resources directly to children, this would not be unattractive, and would eliminate the 'middle' period of child care required by working parents.

As for the other two periods, it is possible that the adoption of flexible working hours would eliminate either the morning or the afternoon need for care. It is clear that the juxtaposition of normal working hours and the classroom day was not arranged with working mothers in mind. But with working mothers now an important segment of the work force, a change would seem in order. In Chapter 2, Table 9, changes in work patterns were the first choice (in the 1973 survey) as a way to improve child care arrangements by almost 60 per cent of working mothers with only school age children. Some firms and institutions in Toronto have experimented quite successfully with allowing employees some flexibility in picking their work hours, so long as the employee is present during a core period of time, for example 9:30 A.M. to 3:00 P.M. (for a more detailed discussion of the experience in Ontario in the last few years with flexible hours, see Robertson and Ferlejowski, 1975). The mother working a seven-hour day could work from 9:30 A.M. to 5:00 P.M., taking thirty minutes for lunch, and require only two and one-half hours of after school care. If school facilities (gyms, cafeterias, classrooms) are used, and assuming ratios of seventeen children per adult, one can imagine costs per child of well under $2 per day.[8] In fact, under flexible working hours, some mothers might choose to work a five-hour day (or even, skipping lunch hour, a six-hour day) and avoid any care arrangements entirely. The provincial government has taken the lead in adopting flexible hours itself and might provide incentives for firms to experiment with this system.

(d) *Day care for infants*

For babies, under age two, it is hard to justify an educational program (although this is not a position subscribed to by all experts). It does not seem unreasonable to expect mothers to lose those few years from the work force, and to divert all public monies to programs for older children. Mothers in high-wage professions could, of course, use day care and deduct the cost from taxable income. It would not be extreme to suggest particular mothers' allowances for parents with young children to enable the mother to stay home during these years. So long as it goes to all parents, it need not be inefficient (nor, in a period of falling birth rates, is it likely to induce unwanted changes in fertility).

THE COSTS OF SUBSIDIZED DAY CARE AND THE BENEFITS

(a) *The costs*

Any subsidized child care program that reaches most Ontario children will be expensive. This is because the cost of day care per child is high, and there are

---

8 Assume one adult half time (at a salary of $5000 per year) for seventeen children, and administration costs of 50 per cent of staff costs. Both are high. This costs $8.82 per child per week.

many children in Ontario. But the cost to the economy of care for children is high whether those children are cared for in the home or in day care centres. A Swedish economist estimated that his country's GNP could be 50 per cent higher if all women worked and were employed at jobs of productivity equal to that of men (Karne et al., 1973). Of course, this gain is illusory, since it neglects the value of production within the household, though in a sense it points out the value of that household production, much of which is child care. When women stay at home and care for children the loss of their productivity in the work force is the cost to society of that child care.

There were 790,383 children under six years of age in Ontario in 1974. If all those children were cared for in day care centres, and assuming one adult for every five children (since one-third of these children are infants, requiring more care, and since the day care 'day' exceeds the work 'day' in length, this would be about the legal minimum staff-to-child ratio), about four and a half per cent of Ontario's 1974 labour force (of three and a half million) would have been required in the day care sector. This would make child care one of Ontario's largest employers (as it is now, if we include day care within the household).

As mentioned earlier, the Province of Ontario spent $11.7 million on day care in 1974. To put this in perspective, consider a universal program for all the children under six years of age in Ontario in 1974. To establish the cost of the universal day care program in 1976, assume the same number of children as in 1974 and assume the use of municipal day care similar to that in Metropolitan Toronto, costing about $2700 for a child aged 2 to 4 years in 1976. Using the assumptions about relative costs for other ages (2.9 times more for children under two, 0.75 times for children age 5), and assuming equal numbers of children in each age category, we come up with a total cost of $3.65 *billion*. This does not include care for children in public school. Even cutting costs to the bone, to generate the annual charges of $1800 per child age 2 to 4 years in some private centre, the bill comes to $2.43 billion,[9] an increase of more than two hundred times the 1974 expenditures. If costs were increased to generate higher quality care, the total figure would naturally be higher.

Even the cost of the voucher system proposed above would be significantly higher than current provincial expenditures on day care. Aimed at children aged 2 to 4 (the five-year olds are already in school part-time), the program would provide two to three hours per day for each child with staff-child ratios of, for example, one to five. Assume an average staff salary of $10,000 in 1976, and

---

9 The same assumptions about the relative costs of younger and older children is made. Since $1800 is two-thirds of the higher cost, the total is also two-thirds of the earlier total cost.

that each staff member would handle three shifts of children. Add on 40 per cent to cover administration, rent, maintenance, etc., and the final cost would be $369 million.[10] If early education is as productive as some predict, the cost is well worth it. But we are talking about a twentyfold increase in provincial expenditures (with no guess as to what portion would be shared by the federal government).

A less universal scheme would cost less. But such a scheme would be hard to sell politically (since it misses most voters). And it would 'ghetto-ize' day care. Day care paid for by the province in 1973-74 cost 'only' $12 million, precisely because it reached very few people. This occurred because only the very poor qualified.

It may be decided that the children of the middle class do not require large subsidies for developmental programs. The voucher discussed earlier could be income tested, with the full voucher going to the very poor and no voucher going to the rich. It is easy to see that this would reduce the cost of subsidies for care, primarily because the total value of the vouchers is less, and in addition because some of the well-off will be less likely to use their 'partial' voucher. The cost can be reduced well below $369 million, but with some loss in the effectiveness of the program. When social services reach only the poor, the community as a whole has little sense of involvement and concern for what is going on. Standards have a tendency to slip, since most voters regard the program as unimportant to their own families. A successful day care program depends on community involvement and concern.

Of course, the voucher scheme might be expected to increase labour force participation. The extra economic activity will generate significant increases in the taxes paid to the federal and provincial governments, which would reduce significantly the net cost to the governments. If as few as five per cent more mothers worked, assuming, of course, that jobs exist for these mothers, and if those mothers earned an average of $7500 each, and paid additional taxes (on both husband's and wife's earnings) of an average of $1500, tax revenues would rise by about $40 million. Even if all these women did not themselves find jobs, supply pressure in the labour market in the long run by low-skill workers might be assumed to generate jobs (at low wages) for others who had been unemployed. This assumes a constant long-run rate of unemployment in the economy.

It is sometimes argued that the day care sector will also generate tax revenues. This, however, is double counting. If some of the mothers entering the labour force for the first time work in day care, then their taxes have already been

10 Three hundred and ninety-five thousand children, one staff member for every 15 children, 40 per cent in non-salary costs, and an average wage of $10,000 are multiplied together to produce 395,000 X (1/15) X 1.4 X $10,000 = $369 million.

counted in the previous paragraph. If day care workers are drawn from other sectors, then they would already have been paying taxes. In fact, if the pay was higher in those other sectors, then it may be necessary to subtract tax revenues.

It may be argued that day care would provide jobs for those trained in education and unable to get jobs in the shrinking public education sector. This would be a short-run justification for a long-term program with very long-term cost implications.

It was also argued that day care should be tax deductible. Changes in the law in 1976 come closer to full deductibility. Ignoring the very significant problem of securing receipts (in a sector that has been largely cash only to evade taxes), it was earlier estimated that 30 per cent of the mothers in 1967 paid for child care, while the average cost of child care in 1973 for those who paid was $19 per week (or $1000 per year). In 1973 there were 452,000 working mothers in Ontario. Assuming an average marginal tax rate of 25 to 30 per cent among these women, with 30 per cent paying an average of $19 for care, full deductibility would have cost between $34 million and $41 million. Of course, any increase in the work force would generate tax revenues to counterbalance this loss.

(b) *Who benefits?*
Quite naturally the distributional effects of a day care program will depend upon the specific structure of the program itself, and, of course, upon the kind of taxes levied to pay for the program. In general, the major impact of the program will be to redistribute income towards families with young children. In the long run, using a lifecycle model of the family, this will benefit large families but not those who prefer to remain childless. It is clear that this is the intent of many day care advocates, who view children as a community responsibility.

Suppose that the program is a universal one paid for out of general revenues. What would be the effect on the income distribution? In a study of senior public kindergartens in 1971, John Buttrick found that the net effect of the benefits and costs of the program (benefits and costs each totalled $28.8 million) was to redistribute about four and a half million dollars from the top quintile to the bottom three quintiles.[11] Since education is partially financed by property taxes, which tend to be more regressive than income taxes, and since day care is much more expensive than kindergarten and affects more children, day care might involve more redistribution. Some comments, however, must be made. The first is that the current income distribution results *in part* from the variation in income over a family's lifecycle. Since young children are generally present when

---

11 The data were provided to the author in November 1976 by John Buttrick, Professor of Economics at York University.

a family is at its worst point financially, looking at redistribution at one particular time would be misleading. Secondly, one must beware of valuing the benefits equally to all families with children (a point which Buttrick himself notes). The benefit of day care (of the kind now provided publicly; that is, of 'minimum' quality, using the HEW classification) to the family depends upon the cost of the alternative arrangements for child care available to the family. If a family has available low-cost care from a reliable neighbour, one can hardly assess the value of free day care at $2700 per year. If the mother's earnings would lead the family to pay no more than $800 for day care (at a higher cost, the mother chooses to stay home), then the value to the family of free day care is only $800. This would seriously reduce the redistributional aspect of any day care program. Middle- and upper-class women with higher earning potential than poor women would place a much higher value on free day care.

It is exactly the fact that many families would value the service of free day care at less than its cost that would make day care a poor way to redistribute income. This raises the last point. It has been assumed that a day care program would be financed by an increase in taxes. If, in fact, day care is financed at the expense of other services, then the impact can be quite perverse. The argument in this chapter has been that there exist far more efficient ways to redistribute income.

DAY CARE, LABOUR FORCE PARTICIPATION, AND FERTILITY

At one extreme, some feel that day care subsidies would have no impact on labour force participation, that the availability of day care has no relationship to the entry of mothers into the labour force (Clifford, 1971). And, in fact, no such relationship has been proven. On the other hand, many researchers accept as fact that inadequate child care serves as a barrier to many mothers entering the labour force. For example, the Statistics Canada Labour Force Survey in 1973 asked mothers who were not working whether they would prefer to work, and if so, what was stopping them. The results are summarized in Table 25. The forty thousand women, who would have worked had suitable child care been available, would increase the number of mothers in the labour force by just under 9 per cent, a not insignificant amount. If we assume, however, that most of those forty thousand mothers stopped from working were parents of pre-school children, then the increase in the labour force of mothers with pre-schoolers would be 24 per cent.

An American study (Ditmore and Prosser, 1973) examined a number of different surveys and found a variety of results. Basically, most surveys found that at least some women claimed that inadequate child care represented a bar to labour force entry. One experiment in Gary seemed to find little immediate impact when day care subsidies were introduced (Ditmore and Prosser, 1973, 32-36).

The variation in opinion can have two roots. The first is one of definition. There can be little doubt that highest quality universal free day care (costing, say, $5000 for a child aged 3 years) would induce many women to enter the labour force. In that sense, women who state that they do not work because of the inadequacy of child care arrangements are simply stating that they are relatively more efficient in the home, *given* the cost of caring for their children. Were *good* day care available free, the judgment not to work looks less efficient.

The two views expressed above — that availability of day care does not affect labour force participation, and that inadequate day care is a barrier to labour force participation — are not contradictory if seen in terms of who is to pay for day care. The first statement suggests that child care markets operate smoothly enough so that a woman willing to pay X dollars per day for child care can most likely find care whose quality is *reasonably* close to the top possible at that price; that is, there are not too many women willing to pay $40 per week for care who are put off from working because of the lack of a functioning market for care in that price range. The second statement suggests that frequently women do not work because the cost of purchasing the desired level of child care exceeds the value to the mother of the time freed by that care, taking into account all the issues discussed earlier — the joint productivity in the home forgone when women work, the future salary benefit obtained by current labour force participation, the psychic benefits of working or not working. If the desired child care were available at low cost, these women would work.

The view that child care availability inhibits labour force participation is also an ideological issue. To many 'modern' individuals, all women *should* want to work. If they do not work, it can only be that day care is inadequate, labour markets are inadequate, and so on. To the extent that this ideology is communicated in some questionnaries, women who choose not to work might find refuge in choosing the phrase 'inadequate child care arrangements' to explain that they really do want to work, but cannot.[12]

The American study discussed above concluded

that the provision of free and adequate day care services to low-income mothers will lead to an increase in labour force participation; in fact, a ten percentage

---

12 The serious student must beware the evidence on day care generated by the large number of surveys using questionnaires. It is almost impossible to avoid having the interviewee use the answers to justify morally a decision in as 'loaded' an area as child care and work for mothers with young children.

point increase (from 32 to 42 percent) in participation [of mothers with children under age six] is estimated. (Ditmore and Prosser, 1973, 1)

Essentially, the report concludes that free and adequate day care would allow us to treat mothers with preschool children as though those children were, in fact, of school age. Since, in general, labour force participation rates increase by about ten percentage points when the youngest child enters school, this yields the increase in the participation rate from 32 to 42 per cent in the quote above.

Unfortunately, this technique has one major flaw. Exactly what is meant by 'adequate' day care? Each mother will set different standards, yet no government program could hope to meet many of those expectations. One might easily suggest that many mothers will agree to work if offered free enriched high-quality day care costing $10,000 per year per child. But this observation is hardly useful in evaluating the increase in labour force participation when day care at a much lower level of quality is made available.

The second root for the difference of opinion is the different measured elasticities for labour force participation of married women, and the different interpretations of the way in which day care can fit into the model of labour force participation. A day care subsidy clearly serves as a work incentive to the target group of parents. Suppose that a mother is considering taking a job that will pay $6000 per year, but that day care while the parent is working would cost $2000 per year. A 50 per cent subsidy to day care would raise the *net* wage to the parent (after day care is paid for) from $4000 to $5000. This would be a work incentive.

But several issues complicate this. First, the subsidy must be financed, unless the work response by mothers is so overwhelming that income tax revenues rise enough to cover the subsidy. If it is financed through additional income taxes on the target group, then the rise in the marginal tax rate will reverse somewhat the work incentive. If the subsidy is financed out of general revenue, then the general rise in tax rates may reduce labour force participation (depending on the slope of the labour supply curve).

Secondly, even if we imagine that the subsidy is financed by a lump sum tax (which reverses all the implications of the earlier model), the structure of the subsidy will influence its effect. Under the current system, where child care to welfare women is subsidized only in municipal or approved private day care centres, the value of the subsidy to the mother may be much less than its dollar cost (a not unusual occurrence with transfers in kind), which significantly reduces the work incentive. This point was made in the previous section, and may be clarified by an example. Suppose that a mother is contemplating working at $6000 per year and paying $2000 for child care for two children in the home of a reliable friend well known to the mother. A day care subsidy that offered $4800 in care in a day care centre to this mother for $1600 (two-thirds subsidy) would not be seen as an increase in the net wage $3200. The mother might well prefer care by her friend. But even if she felt the two types of care were equivalent, the subsidy is worth only $400 to the mother (the cost of care being reduced from $2000 to $1600).[13]

And even if we can agree on the magnitude of the effect on the mother's net wage, there is still significant disagreement as to the elasticity of the mother's labour supply curve. Imagining an arrangement where day care subsidies could be financed through a lump sum tax on the target group of parents (say, by reducing the basic exemption on earned income), we would be interested in the 'pure substitution effect'; that is, the effect on labour force participation of a rise in wage rates, with income compensated (taken away) so as to leave the family no richer. But Glen Cain and Harold Watts review six studies of the 'pure substitution elasticity' and find estimates running from 2.5 to about zero (Cain and Watts, 1973, 336-337).

Assume an elasticity of 1.2 and a voucher system as proposed above. Assume that the voucher would subsidize about 30 per cent of the care purchased by the average parent, and that full deductibility would increase the subsidy rate to 50 per cent. Assume further that the program is paid for either by lump sum taxes on the target group or by non-distortionary (!) taxes on the general economy. Assume that care now costs the average parent about $1000 annually. Assume finally an average after tax wage rate of $8000 facing the target group of women in the province (this is high). Then the subsidy would change the net wage from $7000 to $7500, an increase of 7.1 per cent. With an elasticity of 1.2, labour force participation would rise by 8.5 per cent. If the wage rate is taken as $6000, the increase would be 12 per cent. Since 169 thousand Ontario mothers with preschoolers worked in 1973, this would increase the labour force by between fourteen thousand and twenty thousand people. Under the same assumptions, universal free day care would double the subsidy and bring between twenty-eight and forty thousand mothers of preschoolers into the labour force.

The estimates are entirely arbitrary. Greater accuracy will depend on better estimates of elasticities for mothers contemplating entering the work force. It should be noted that a high elasticity would increase significantly the tax revenue earned by the government, and cover at least part of the cost of the program.

Finally, what would be the effect on fertility of absorption by the state of the cost of much of day care. At first glance, the response might be that subsidy

13 For work on labour force participation which tries to take account of the real value to the family of free day care, see Heckman (1974).

must *increase* fertility, since it reduces the cost of children (and demand curves slope downwards). Theoretically, this is not so. The production of the 'child services' in the model in the Appendix to Chapter 4 said nothing about the number of children. Child services can be increased by raising the number of children or by raising the resources used per child, and studies seem to indicate that parents prefer the latter.[14] In any case, it was suggested that there might well be little change in the relative welfare of children and adult enjoyment when prices changed (income held constant).

In this last case, assume that the family's enjoyment of children is to be constant. Then a fall in the price of day care makes work more attractive. But while staying at home, the cost of additional children is not linear – the major cost to the parent is the first child (in terms of loss of freedom and time). Further children absorb less extra time and cost. However, in a day care centre extra children do cost more. Working may thus induce parents to have fewer children and spend more on each one. The mathematical argument is sketched out in Appendix B.

Thus, a subsidy can affect fertility in either way. More women will begin to work and tend to have smaller families; those already working may choose to enjoy children more and have larger families.

CONCLUSION

The current day care policy in Ontario violates the criteria for efficiency set up in the previous chapter. Free day care to low-income families induces some parents to enter the labour force when economic factors make entry inefficient. Subsidies that pay only for institutional day care lead families to use the highest cost form of extra-family child care.

To help families, a wage subsidy would be far more efficient. It seems that day care has been seized upon as a popular issue on which to fight for income redistribution to families with children (especially poorer families). To some extent this is a 'women's issue.' Current tax law treats harshly the second earner in a two-parent family. Yet the multiplicity of tasks performed by the women in the household makes the real gain to the family when she works much less than the wage rate (the economist might argue that the real problem is that production in the household is not taxed). With more mothers working, an attempt is being made to reduce the tax rate on the second earner, and day care

---

14 See the various discussions in *New Economic Approaches to Fertility,* Proceedings of a Conference June 8-9, 1972, *Journal of Political Economy,* vol. 81, no. 2, Pt. II, March/April 1973. In particular, see Willis (1973), Michael (1973), and Becker and Lewis (1973).

subsidies represent the focus of this attempt. But merely demonstrating that day care subsidies are less efficient than tax rate reductions does not resolve the issue of redistribution.

It is also not clear that full subsidies to day care are the best way to reach children with special assistance. It seems more likely that a part-day enriched program would be most efficient. A voucher scheme was proposed to reach children irrespective of whether or not their parents worked and used institutional day care.

Day care is a very emotional issue. This must not lead the analyst into errors of logic. Inefficient programs that fail to deal adequately with the very problems they were designed to solve and that will waste limited resources must be avoided.

TABLE 21

Family income under family benefits as earned income rises

Weeks of work	Hours worked per week	Wage rate per hour	Employment income	Family benefits allowance	Other benefits*	Income taxes	Charge to family for day care	Total income plus benefits, minus day care charge	Implicit marginal tax rate on earnings (%)
0	–	–	0	3936	2678	0	0	6614	0
10	30	$2.40	720	3936	2678	0	0	7334	25
20	30	$2.40	1440	3756	2678	0	0	7874	75
50	30	$2.40	3600	2136	2678	0	0	8414	289
50	36	$2.40	4320	0	2983	252	0	7051	63
50	36	$2.80	5040	0	2749	425	45	7319	74
50	36	$6.00	10,800	0	1127	1637	1489	8801	

*Include rent subsidies, OHIP premium subsidies, family allowance, tax credit, but *not* day care subsidies.
SOURCE: Ontario Economic Council, 1976, 26

TABLE 22

Family income under a 'notch-less' family benefits program, with a guarantee of $6500, no other benefits, a tax-back rate of 75% (or an income exemption of 25%), day care costs of $2000: a comparison of: (A) day care charged under needs test, income exemption of $1200 in all calculations and (B) day care deductible for computing tax back of income, income exemption of $1866.67

Weeks of work (35 hour week)	Wage rate per hour	Employment income	Scheme A			Scheme B		
			Total benefits (net of income tax)	Charge for day care (%)	Total income after day care	Total benefits (net of income tax)	Charge for day care	Total income after day care
0	—	0	$6500	0	$ 6500	$6500	0	$ 6500
10	$2.40	$ 840	6500	0	7340	6500	$ 400	6940
20	2.40	1680	6140	0	7820	6500	800	7380
30	2.40	2520	5510	0	8030	6500	1200	7820
50	2.40	4200	4250	0	8450	6250	2000	8450
50	3.00	5250	3463	0	8713	5463	2000	8713
50	3.60	6300	2675	0	8975	4675	2000	8975
50	4.20	7350	1888	0	9238	3888	2000	9238
50	4.80	8400	1100	0	9500	3100	2000	9500
50	5.40	9450	800	487	9763	2313	2000	9763
50	6.00	10,500	800	1275	10,025	1525	2000	10,025
50	6.60	11,550	738	2000	10,288	738	2000	10,288
50	7.20	12,600	−50	2000	10,550	−50	2000	10,550

TABLE 23

Family income under a 'notch-less' family benefits program, with a guarantee of $6500, no other benefits, a tax-back rate of 75%, and day care costs of $4800, a comparison of: (A) day care charged under needs test, income exemption of $1200 on all calculations and (B) day care deductible for computing tax back of income, income exemption of $2800

Weeks of work (35 hour week)	Wage rate per hour	Employment income	Scheme A			Scheme B		
			Total benefits (net of income tax)	Charge for day care ($)	Total income after day care	Total benefits (net of income tax)	Charge for day care	Total income after day care
0	—	0	$6500	0	$ 6500	$6500	0	$ 6500
10	$2.40	$ 840	6500	0	7340	6500	$ 960	6380
20	2.40	1680	6140	0	7820	6500	1920	6260
30	2.40	2520	5510	0	8030	6500	2880	6140
50	2.40	4200	4250	0	8450	6500	4800	5900
50	3.00	5250	3463	0	8713	6500	4800	6950
50	3.60	6300	2675	0	8975	6500	4800	8000
50	4.20	7350	1888	0	9238	6500	4800	9050
50	4.80	8400	1100	0	9500	5900	4800	9500
50	5.40	9450	800	487	9763	5113	4800	9763
50	6.00	10,500	800	1275	10,025	4325	4800	10,025
50	6.60	11,550	800	2062	10,288	3538	4800	10,288
50	7.20	12,600	800	2850	10,550	2750	4800	10,550
50	7.80	13,650	800	3637	10,813	1963	4800	10,813

TABLE 24

Family income, under day care subsidy, for family of five with two adults and $8500 in family budget under needs test, $750 exemption plus 25% of net income exempt

Husband's net earnings (after taxes)	Wife's net earnings (after taxes)	Cost of day care	Charge for day care	Family income (after paying for day care)
$ 4000	0	0	0	$ 4000
$ 4000	$ 4000	$2400	0	$ 8000
$ 4000	$ 6000	$2400	0	$10,000
$ 4000	0	0	0	$ 4000
$ 4000	$ 4000	$4800	0	$ 8000
$ 4000	$ 6000	$4800	0	$10,000
$ 6000	0	0	0	$ 6000
$ 6000	$ 4000	$4800	0	$10,000
$ 6000	$ 6000	$4800	0	$12,000
$ 8000	0	0	0	$ 8000
$ 8000	$ 4000	$4800	0	$12,000
$ 8000	$ 6000	$4800	$1250	$12,750
$ 8000	$ 8000	$4800	$2750	$13,250
$10,000	0	0	0	$10,000
$10,000	$ 4000	$4800	$1250	$12,750
$10,000	$ 6000	$4800	$2750	$13,250
$10,000	$ 8000	$4800	$4250	$13,750
$10,000	$10,000	$4800	$4800	$15,200

TABLE 25

Reasons for not working by mothers in Canada and Ontario, 1973

Reason for not working	Canada		Ontario	
	Number in thousands	%	Number in thousands	%
Believed no suitable work available	89	24	28	25
Cannot make satisfactory child care arrangements	149	40	40	36
Other reasons	136	36	42	38
Total	375	100	110	100

SOURCE: Statistics Canada, Labour Force Survey Division, 1975, 85-86

APPENDIX B: THE IMPACT OF DAY CARE
SUBSIDIZATION ON FERTILITY

Use the model developed in some length in the Appendix in Chapter 4. If C is constant, then the only relevant conditions for a maximum arise from the suboptimization problem:

$$\text{minimize } P_{XC}X_C + P_T T_C \text{ subject to } g(X_C, T_C) = \bar{C}. \tag{54}$$

To bring in number of children, assume that N, the number of children is chosen, for any level of X_C and T_C, so as to maximize child services, where child services is a function of N and Q, the quality of care per child. Thus define

$$g(X_C, T_C) = \underset{N}{\text{maximum }} C[Q, N], \tag{55}$$

where

$$Q = h(X_C, T_C, N). \tag{56}$$

These three equations generate a solution for X_C, T_C, and N. Now if day care is subsidized, X_C will rise and T_C will fall. If child services are kept constant, then we may show that

$$\left. \frac{dN}{dX_C} \right|_{g=\bar{C}} = \frac{\left[h_{TN} - h_{XN} \dfrac{P_T}{P_{XC}} \right] C_Q}{C_{QQ} h_N^2 + 2C_{QN} h_N + C_Q h_{NN} + C_{NN}}, \tag{57}$$

where $J_K = \partial J / \partial K$ and $J_{KL} = \partial^2 J / \partial K \partial L$ for $J = C$ or h, and K or $L = Q, N, X$ or T. It may be shown that

$$\left. \frac{dN}{dX_C} \right|_{g=\bar{C}}$$

is negative if

$$\frac{Q_{XN}}{P_{XC}} < \frac{Q_{TN}}{P_T}.$$

Now Q_{XN} is the change in the marginal productivity of goods in producing child quality as number of children rises, while Q_{TN} is the change in marginal product of time in producing quality as number of children rises. Both are negative. If increases in the number of children 'dilutes' goods more than it does time (in reaching children), then the number of children will decline as more goods are used.

6

Public policy and the provision of day care: intervention on the supply side

INTRODUCTION

Wherever day care centres have developed, some government regulation has been present. At first it has tended to be only the supervision of fire and safety standards. But invariably, growth of the sector has brought calls for increased public overview of the quality of care being provided. There seems a general distrust by many in the day care field of the free and unregulated operation of the marketplace. Economists tend to dismiss much of current regulation as serving the economic interests of those already in the sector at the expense of the consumer. But in the day care area, demands for regulation have come from many professionals outside the market who are deeply concerned about the kind of care received by children.

Day care is seen by many as an endeavour ill-suited to the common practices of profit-maximizing commercial entrepreneurs. But for most goods, public policy relies primarily on the judgments of consumers to control what firms produce. The profit motive is in many cases a positive feature, leading firms to respond quickly to the wishes of consumers. What makes day care different? The following section examines the reasons why day care firms seeking only to maximize profits might fail to meet the needs of parents, and why particular characteristics of the day care market prevent consumers from effectively eliminating undesirable firms from the industry. Some of the alternatives to the free market system of providing day care are then looked at. Different institutional forms – the non-profit centre, the public centre, the co-operative –

are examined, and attention is paid to the possibility of regulating commerical centres. Following this is a description of the way the day care industry has evolved in Ontario and how it has been controlled. Some modifications to current policies are suggested. Finally, the findings of this chapter are summarized.

THE FREE MARKET AS A MECHANISM OF CONTROL –
THE PARTICULAR CASE OF DAY CARE

(a) *Consumer sovereignty as a control on quality*

For most economists, the quality of output of most products is not a concern of public policy. In the traditional model of consumer choice, consumers are assumed to have perfect knowledge of the quality of the goods arrayed before them in the marketplace. Producers supplying inferior products at the going price simply do not exist, since consumers will not patronize such producers. But even when this assumption of perfect information is relaxed, the market can still function efficiently. The consumer may not know whether or not the plump shiny apple on the grocer's shelf really tastes as good as it looks, but the consumer will soon find out. And grainy or sour apples will result in few repeat sales for that brand, or even that grocer, if the produce is uniformly bad. Low-quality items (at high-quality prices) disappear from the marketplace, and, unless they learn quickly, so do the producers of those items.

In recent years, some people have become uncomfortable with this stylized view of the market and of the power of the consumer. For example, Akerlof (1970) suggests that when sellers have much more information about quality than buyers, low-quality goods will masquerade as higher-quality goods and the market mechanism can be destroyed (the fall in quality drives the price down, in turn eliminating many high-quality producers from the market). Spence (1972) suggests that when an item is difficult to evaluate, sellers will attempt to acquire characteristics (called signals) that buyers associate with high quality, whether or not those characteristics have any value to consumers. In discussing medical care, Arrow suggests that potential difficulties arise in a market system whenever producers know much more about the quality of their product than do consumers:

... the difference in information relevant here is a difference in information as to the consequence of a purchase of medical care. There is always an inequality of information as to production methods between the producer and the purchaser of any commodity, but in most cases the customer may well have as good or nearly as good an understanding of the utility of the product as the producer. (Arrow, 1963, 951-2)

Day care is one sector in which the distrust of the market might be justified, where producers might well know more about the quality of the service than do consumers. This is true for a number of reasons. The purchaser of the service – the parent – is not after all the direct consumer. The parent may see the day care centre (or babysitter) briefly in the morning and evening, but the care is administered while the parent is at work. And the preschool child is not easily able to inform his parent of the true quality of the care he is receiving, nor indeed could the child necessarily evaluate that care (the extent of developmental programming, for example). Aside from some obvious physical characteristics of the centre (clean washrooms, bright toys) and the absence of obvious child abuse, there are few easily observable characteristics that might enable the parent to judge good day care. A day care professional may well be able to enter a day care centre and judge within a short period of time the quality of the care provided. It is harder to imagine an untrained parent doing the same thing.

The market model can tolerate bad judgments by consumers, so long as those consumers can gradually learn to discern high quality correctly. But in day care, by the time the parent has developed some ability to judge, the child might well have grown older and left the centre. And any 'damage' done by the centre might not become apparent for years. Even when parents are able to form rapid judgments of the day care received by their children, these parents may not want to jump around among centres too much, for fear that the frequent changes in environment may hurt the children.

Hirschman (1970) suggests that economists have overemphasized the power of 'exit' and underestimated the power of 'voice' as a control on the action of the firm. 'Exit' is the removal by the consumer of his patronage from the inferior supplier, while 'voice' refers to more direct attempts by the consumer to influence quality, for example by complaints to the management of the firm, by political demands for regulation, by action to arouse other consumers, etc. A little exit, suggests Hirschman, is not necessarily a good thing, since it siphons off the most perceptive consumers, leaving behind the less vocal and aware majority. This would occur where the firm is a monopolist, or where all oligopolists[1] simultaneously reduce quality.

But Hirschman's observations can be extended further to a competitive market. So long as a rapid turnover of consumers of child care ensures that inferior centres (inferior in the sense that they provide less desirable care at the same price as other centres) will replace most of those who exit with less

1 For the non-economist, we can define an oligopolist as one of a small number of firms dominating a market, and a monopolist as a single firm dominating a market.

informed newcomers, exit will fail to eliminate the firm. A model of this process has been developed elsewhere by the author of this report (Krashinsky, 1973). Without repeating that analysis, in detail, the model can be summarized here.

Consumers are assumed to enter the market for day care with an imperfect ability to choose among the 'good' and 'bad' day care centres available in the market. Each period a number of consumers leave the market entirely (their children grow up) and a number of new consumers enter the market. Those consumers who remain acquire some additional knowledge of quality and some additional ability to evaluate the relative quality of the centre currently used and the other centres in the area. On the supply side, centres enter the market to provide either 'good' or 'bad' quality (at the going uniform price), with entry occurring at rates suitable to keep all economic profits equal to zero. Naturally, good centres will enjoy greater patronage than bad centres, since new consumers have some ability to discriminate, and each period some experienced consumers switch from bad to good centres. This greater patronage for good centres results in lower vacancy rates (excess capacity) in good centres. But bad quality centres are able to tolerate higher excess capacity and still not lose money because bad centres are more profitable than good centres when both arc full. This higher profitability is the result of the cost cutting that leads to lower quality.

It may be shown that perfect information is not required to eliminate all bad centres, but that at some point, as information and the ability to judge centres by consumers is reduced, bad centres will exist in equilibrium. If consumers, both new and experienced, become less able to differentiate between bad and good quality, more bad centres will survive. And if bad centres are allowed in the model to cut costs even more before they are classified as 'bad', then their profitability when full will increase, and again more bad centres will exist in the market. Finally, the more consumer choice is limited by other considerations (the high value consumers place on using a centre close to home, for example), the easier it will be for bad centres to survive.

Clearly, exit will not be effective if the information consumers have about day care is as bad as has been suggested earlier in this chapter. And encouraging exit may be counter-productive if it removes from bad centres the very consumers who are perceptive and active enough to exercise voice (by organizing other consumers to confront those running the day care centre, for example).

(b) *Can the market adapt to poor information?*
It should be pointed out that not all economists would agree with this evaluation of the market. It is, after all, easy to argue that consumers in fact know very little about most things that are purchased. How many consumers know exactly what engineering goes into each car, exactly what tolerances and safety factors

are allowed? Yet the public is willing to allow the market to operate freely in most sectors. And even where information is poor, the market provides ways to improve consumer control. Brand names develop, so that one manufacturer guarantees the integrity of many different products, thus supposedly increasing the incentive for a manufacturer to raise quality, since losing a customer for one product likely loses him for all. Consumers exchange information, providing new consumers with a 'grapevine' full of information about the various producers. And producers exploit this by franchising, ensuring uniform quality among all producers bearing the name of the franchise.

These adaptations do not reassure many in the day care field. Day care is by its nature a decentralized commodity, with quality dependent to a great degree upon the individual staff within a centre and the guidance they receive from their supervisors. It is hard to imagine the kind of quality control by a central authority that is possible in a chain of motels or of fried chicken outlets.

In the past, child care has generally been provided within the extended family. The decision not to purchase child care in the marketplace but to produce it oneself was, as discussed earlier, motivated largely by the relative efficiency of work in the home and market. But there has also been a deep reluctance by parents to entrust the care of a child to those who might not share either the parents' deep concern for the welfare of the child or the parents' views on what kind of upbringing is best for the child. And it is voice, not exit, that controls the quality of care within the family.

Economic theory of the firm suggests that in many activities firms perform a function themselves, rather than going to the market where other more specialized firms can perform the same function slightly more efficiently. This is because the firm believes that its employees are more easily controlled and more likely to act in the best interests of the firm than would another enterprise, bound to it only by the *quid pro quo* relationship of a contract.

As the extended family has shrunk and as relative efficiencies have changed, the family has turned to the market for its commodities. But until recently, this trend has been resisted in child care. This suggests that voice is a far more effective tool than exit for controlling quality in this sector. And the distrust of the marketplace may help explain the preference by parents for care by friends or relatives over care in a day care centre.

The view one hears when talking to professionals in day care is that it 'should not' be dominated by the profit motive. In part, this represents the natural taste of those committed to the highest quality care for children (as will be seen, non-profit enterprises tend to offer products too high in quality). In part, it represents the current tendency to blame business and the profit motive for all that is wrong with society. But at least in some measure, the fear of for-profit centres is based on a suspicion that unscrupulous firms might be able to exploit parents and damage children in a sector where exit is not particularly effective.

Day care is not the only sector in which the profit motive is suspect. We might feel nervous about going to a doctor whose sole concern was his bank balance. Society protects itself by making out of the doctor-patient relationship more than just an exchange of dollars. A code of ethics, a sense of professionalism is relied upon to impose limits other than exit on the profits of the doctor. In other sectors, more closely related to day care, profit seeking has also been suspect. In the area of nursing homes, proprietory institutions have had very mixed reviews. And in education, society has turned to non-profit institutions rather than tolerate the activities of for-profit firms.

But if the profit maximizing firm is not ideally suited to day care, neither necessarily is any other type of institution. As shall be seen below, other ways of providing care also suffer liabilities. In the economist's view, the for-profit day care centres, whatever their other faults, do have some very desirable characteristics. For-profit firms generally respond sharply to increases in demand, expanding at the lure of increased sales (and profits). For-profit firms operate efficiently, cutting costs to the bone to maximize profits. For-profit centres respond quickly to changes in tastes among parents, to win new customers and expand profits.

While one may not be entirely willing to trust a day care sector made up only of for-profit firms, it may still be true that some profit-making firms represent a healthy addition to the industry.

ALTERNATIVES TO THE MARKET – THE NON-PROFIT CENTRE, THE PUBLIC CENTRE, THE CO-OPERATIVE CENTRE, AND THE REGULATED PROPRIETORY CENTRE

(a) *The non-profit day care centre*
One alternative to the profit motive is the centre run by a non-profit agency. It should be noted that in Ontario many centres that are officially commercial actually function as non-profit firms. The designation 'non-profit' is granted to centres that are entitled to solicit funds from the public. But many commercial operators have no profit goals beyond a fair return for the operator's time, and try to provide the highest quality care possible to consumers. In this section the use of the term non-profit will reflect the motives of those running the centre, not the legal designation.

The absence of the profit motive implies no incentive by centre operators to cut costs at the expense of the consumer, preventing the abuses possible in a for-profit centre, although it is possible that the professionals in the centre and the parent will disagree about what constitutes good care. It is thus possible for the child to receive what the parents consider bad care – many parents, for example, hold views of the role of order and discipline that are quite different form those held by professionals in the day care field.

But even ignoring differences of opinion, it is not clear that non-profit centres will operate efficiently. Newhouse, writing about non-profit institutions, suggests that they tend to produce greater quality at greater cost than consumers (in this case, the parents whose children use day care) want (Newhouse, 1970). While Newhouse was writing about monopoly institutions, it remains true that non-profit day care centres subsidized by charities will try to use the subsidy to raise quality (which meets the needs of the professionals running the centre) rather than expand the number of spaces available to the public. The parents who cannot find room in these centres are forced to make alternative arrangements that may well be inferior. Without doubt, some of the best day care centres in Canada are run by charities, even discounting those oriented mainly towards 'multi-problem' families. Whether the community would be better off with slightly lower quality and more spaces is exactly the point.

Perhaps the most serious problem in relying upon the non-profit firm is that the centre has no incentive to expand, quite aside from problems in acquiring funds for expansion, when faced with excess demand. Over-subscribed centres add waiting lists, not spaces. In the economists' profit maximizing world, successful firms expand and eliminate the inefficient. But if successful centres do not grow, then parents must make do with centres that are less efficient or less responsive to the needs of the family. This is a particular problem when the demand for day care is expanding, as it is now.

One non-profit centre operator[2] who spoke with the author served about seventy-five children, and had a waiting list with thirty names on it. The operator estimated that the wait would average four to six months, but commented that, at times, names remained on her waiting list for up to a year. This suggests that the centre is indeed an attractive one, but makes one wonder about the fate of those on the waiting list. The operator felt that she could not do as good a job by expanding and accepting more children and hiring more staff.

(b) *Publicly supplied day care*

Another alternative is the publicly run day care centres. Such a system could be financed through taxes, although for now assume that parents are charged full

2 The centre, which will remain anonymous, was a commercial centre, run by an operator, on salary, who reinvested any profits in upgrading supplies and equipment. The author judged the centre's orientation to be non-profit (quality care, subject to meeting all expenses, including the operator's salary).

fees. Consumers can trust public centres not to turn a large profit at the expense of the children.

However, public agencies tend to be slow to change in response to consumer tastes. If the tastes of the consumer and centre operator differ, there is no economic incentive to change. At present some debate is going on in Ontario on exactly this issue with respect to the public school system. Nor are public centres likely to be as fast as for-profit entrepreneurs to respond to increases in demand, since funds for expansion come through the political process. And without the profit motive, centre operators may have little incentive to hold down costs. This is especially true when day care is paid for through tax revenues.

There has been some discussion about providing a degree of choice among public firms to consumers, especially in the case of public schools; see, for example, Downs (1970). But in order for this choice to be effective, local day care centre directors would have to have some incentive to attract consumers (analogous to the higher profits that drive the competitive model) and be able to expand their facilities if they are successful or cut back if they fail. And this kind of incentive structure embedded in a decentralized public enterprise is quite unknown in the public sector. In fact, it resembles non-profit or for-profit care more than it does public enterprise care.

(c) *Co-operative Day Care*

It is also possible to provide day care through co-operatives, which have grown rapidly in Canada in the last few years. It is important to point out that co-operatives in Canada include all non-profit centres with a plurality on the board of directors of parents with children in the centre. The pure form of co-operative, the 'producer co-operative' in which parents themselves provide all the supervision of the children, is comparatively rare outside of college campuses. This is because few parents have the flexibility in their work schedules that will enable coverage of all hours in the day. And the problems of running a large group with no clear lines of authority can be overwhelming.

The more common 'consumer co-operative' involves care by hired professionals in centres run by the parents. The goal of parental involvement is a worthy one, and can avoid some of the unresponsiveness of an existing non-profit centre run only by professionals. But many parents may have neither the time, the experience, nor the inclination to run their own centres. It is not clear that those parents who do come forward will be willing to take on the responsibility for those who do not. Nor is it clear that the non-participants always will feel themselves particularly well served by the activist parents who do choose to run the centres. A smooth working co-operative will depend upon a certain amount of agreement among parents as to the goals and approaches of the centre, an agreement not always easily achieved. This difficulty in assembling a co-operative might imply that while co-operatives are a valuable part of the day care sector, other types of firms will be required.

(d) Regulation

Finally, it is not necessary to eliminate all for-profit centres. One frequently employed method of controlling the abuses of the profit system in day care (and elsewhere) is regulation. Ideally, a public body protects consumers by inspecting all day care centres and licensing only those that meet established standards. In practice, regulation in most sectors of the economy has not been a device looked on with favour by economists (see, for example, Trebilcock, 1976, and some of the readings in MacAvoy, 1970). It is felt that the regulators frequently end up serving the interests of the very firms they are regulating. In fact, the Day Nurseries Branch in Ontario has worked with centres to raise standards and improve the day care reaching children (Canadian Council on Social Development, 1972, 5-6). But there are other reasons to believe that licensing will not be effective in improving the welfare of children.

The first problem is that licensing, as it is currently practised in Ontario, can only protect families intending to buy day care in one particular price range. There is no specific good called 'day care,' but a whole range of care from minimal custodial care up to expensive individualized care. In Ontario, the basic standard for care implies that day care must cost at least $1700 to $1800 per year (staff must be paid, food bought, etc.). Families purchasing care for that amount are ensured that the care meets minimum standards. But families that can afford to purchase more expensive care enjoy no such protection. Care costing $3000 per year will easily meet standards set for $1800 care without necessarily being the kind of care that $3000 should buy. On the other hand, parents who cannot afford $1800 per year are protected right out of any day care at all.

This last point is not uncommon in society. Laws frequently prohibit transactions that might involve harm to one of the parties. Okun writes that these bans on 'trades of last resort' — trades that someone would undertake only when in dire circumstances — also imply some commitment to eventually ensure that society will prevent the need for those trades (Okun, 1975, 19-22). Society wishes to ensure that children will receive a minimum level of care. But, unfortunately, day care is only one way in which children are cared for. Making unavailable for purchase bare minimum custodial day care (for, say, $1000 per year) may force the parent to stay home, in which case the child *may* receive better care. But more likely the parent will make alternate arrangements that are inferior even to the unavailable low-quality day care. Applying Okun's statement, a ban on low-quality day care logically should be accompanied by either a generous guaranteed income to ensure that all parents can afford care or a subsidy to day care to assist parents in buying care that meets the licensing standards. Day care is subsidized for some children in much of Ontario, but the subsidies do not reach high enough up the income distribution to ensure adequate care for all.

The second problem is that in order to license day care it is necessary to write down on paper exactly what is required of the day care centre. Clearly, it is possible to set standards for safety and for food. But the essential part of day care is the staff itself. We would like to require that all day care staff be loving, committed, skilled individuals who enjoy being with children. That is, of course, impossible to spell out in the legislation. Experienced day care professionals can usually tell after one hour in a day care centre just what kind of care is being provided in the centre, but specifying that judgment in order to provide due process for any centre denied a licence is not practical.

In fact, licensing requirements can only set staff-child ratios and the minimum qualifications of the staff. Some qualifications – an absence of communicable diseases or dangerous mental illness – make good sense. But beyond this, it is not clear what easily measurable qualifications in fact determine the child care abilities of a potential day care worker. Frequently, certain training is required, with high educational degrees necessary for supervisory positions. This might disqualify many individuals who would make excellent day care workers with a minimum of expert supervision. And professional requirements restrict the supply of day care workers, raising their wages, and further increasing the cost of day care. Finally, even if the qualifications were accurate measures of ability, setting both the minimum quality of the staff and the minimum adult-to-child ratio would imply that the best mix of quality and quantity in producing day care is known, whereas in a sector as young as day care, there is certainly room for experimentation. For example, a licensing requirement for a centre of fifty preschool children might require a minimum of eight full-time staff as well as a supervisor with an advanced degree. But, in fact, it may turn out that the centre would function better either with fewer but more qualified staff, or with more full-time staff (including, perhaps, many para-professionals) and no qualified supervisor. Assume, in this case, that either arrangement would cost the same. Also, as was pointed out earlier, a flat ratio of staff to children ignores the varied requirements of different groups of children at different times of the day.

The final problem in licensing is the cost of licensing itself. This occurs not only in the cost of the licensing authority, but also in the cost to the centres of the paperwork required and the cost of the numerous standards that must be met.

THE EVOLUTION OF DAY CARE PROVISION IN ONTARIO: A PROPOSAL

(a) *Licensing and the provision of day care*

Ontario does license day care and sets strict staff-child ratios as laid out in Chapter 3. However, as was pointed out, the issue of licensing in Ontario is confused by the issue of subsidy. Since Ontario subsidizes day care at its minimum standard level, any proposed change in staff ratios is viewed – correctly – as an attempt to alter the level of subsidy. This would affect the quality of most of the day care in the province, since many private centres have agreed to purchase-of-service contracts with the regional governments in Ontario.

Aside from the subsidy question, the staffing standards face all the difficulties described above. By restricting the level of care available, many parents ineligible for subsidy use alternative arrangements that are inferior to the low-quality day care that is not now available. All centres comply with the letter of the law – certainly the quality of care in Ontario centres is quite variable.

Nor is it entirely clear exactly which staff ratios are sufficient. The intense uproar over the changes introduced by Margaret Birch was oriented towards the erosion of the provincial subsidy. Unfortunately, it is not yet entirely clear what the long-run effects of changing staff ratios will be.

The experience in other countries is not particularly useful in forming policy. In Finland, twenty-five children require only one teacher and one trainee (Eskula, 1973). In Sweden one adult supervises five preschoolers (Karne et al., 1973). In Japan, one teacher only is required for thirty children aged four (Takahashi, 1973).

In the rest of Canada, not all provinces have set ratios, although most do license day care centres, requiring fire and safety precautions.[3] British Columbia and Manitoba do not specify ratios, though Winnipeg does. New Brunswick requires one adult for every five children aged two and three years, and one adult for every ten children aged four and five years. Newfoundland and Prince Edward Island are in the process of defining ratios. Alberta requires one adult per twenty children aged two to seven (with a recommended change to one adult to ten children).

Ontario has not restricted any of the possible modes of providing day care. Although Ontario has a significant number of public day care centres, the municipalities undertake agreements with both commercial and non-profit centres. The sector has evolved much as would be anticipated. The non-profit centres include those that are the best in the province and are invariably over-

---

3 The facts that follow are derived from communications with the day care offices in each province.

subscribed. The municipal centres maintain reasonably uniform standards and pay the highest salaries in the province in the field. The commercial centres include two types: small local centres run by individual entrepreneurs, and large centres, many of which are run by single large corporations (for example, Miniskools, an international day care corporation with a number of large centres in Toronto). The proprietary centres tend to pay the lowest salaries, cut costs to the bone, and have the highest number of unsubsidized parents.

There is significant resentment among day care professionals towards Miniskools, Educare, and other large day care corporations. This is not surprising. These firms are dedicated profit maximizers, enrolling their centres to the legal limit and, as was observed earlier, the legal limit is somewhat ambiguous, since it does not specify whether staff ratios are based on enrolment or actual attendance. Some private centres measure ratios in terms of attendance, allowing them to enroll more children. The firms also keep staff salaries as low as possible, and run large centres to take advantage of every economy of scale. Many of the staff earn the minimum wage, and salary increments occur only as staff members assume positions of greater responsibility.[4] However, since most parents in the corporation day care centres pay the full fee, it is not clear that this cost cutting would meet any opposition from consumers. In all likelihood, Miniskools and other like firms serve in the province as a limiting force on the tendency of costs in non-profit and public centres to escalate continually. As we observe, non-profit and public operators do not face profit constraints and have a desire to raise quality, a goal not necessarily shared by parents paying full cost. The regional manager of one firm[5] suggests that most of the opposition to his centres comes not from parents but from professionals.

In fact, the lowest quality day care in the province is not in corporate enterprises but in some of the less responsible smaller proprietary centres. Miniskools and Educare are like the 'brand name' companies we discussed earlier, having to maintain some standards to protect their reputations. And profits of one firm whose books were examined are not large by any measure, totalling about 6 per cent on total revenue in one centre examined by the author, although of course it is possible for any corporation to move profits around within its accounts.

This is not to support the corporate day care centre as a model for day care in the province. In fact, the growing and evolving day care sector in Ontario is probably best served by a multiplicity of institutional forms. Can one say for

4 If one were being cynical, as are some of the people running Miniskools, one could suggest that the low salaries paid to day care workers has some influence on professionals evaluating the care in Miniskool centres.

5 Al Brewer at Miniskools.

certain that the large centres run by Miniskools are not the most efficient form of care? Or that all workers in centres must be paid high wages for the sector to work efficiently? Perhaps the higher quality public centres have the extra resources to develop new programs that could be of use to other centres. Or perhaps the smaller non-profit co-operative centres will prove more responsive to the needs of parents.

As was suggested earlier, each mode of provision has some drawbacks. Together, some of these drawbacks may cancel out. For-profit centres have a tendency to cut quality in invisible ways to raise profits, to maximize not quality but apparent quality. But this tendency is limited when there is visible to the public the large number of municipal and non-profit centres offering care of known quality. The parent has a benchmark — the public centre — with which to compare any private centre.

On the other hand, non-profit and public day care centres have a tendency to raise costs and quality, against the interests of the parents paying full fee and the taxpayers paying any subsidies. The commercial centres, which must sell many of their spaces at full cost to parents, keep costs down, and serve as a base against which taxpayers can compare costs in public centres.

Public centres do not respond to variations in consumer tastes within a region, or to changes in parental wishes. The commercial centres are more responsive, since they must sell their spaces. Public and non-profit centres do not expand quickly when there are increases in demand; commercial entrepreneurs do. Co-operative centres are particularly responsive to parental needs. Other forms fill in for parents who do not wish to spend the time to organize or participate in a co-operative.

Ontario will best be served by a continuation of the current variation in the provision of day care. Each mode serves to some extent to check the excesses of the others. Each mode explores avenues for the future that are not the concern of the others.

(b) *Openness as an alternative to licensing*
On the issue of regulation, it is first necessary to separate out the debate on the level of subsidization from that on regulation. This done, this report would argue that detailed regulation of staff-child ratios and qualifications is of little use in controlling real quality and is actually counterproductive (by discouraging innovation and experimentation). For example, a large producer co-operative with no qualified supervisor might not turn out to be appropriate, but might be worthy of a try. Yet such an experiment might not receive a licence. Neither would a capital intensive centre, employing a multiplicity of media and a limited number of staff. It may turn out that some day care could be provided at low

cost for school children (or preschoolers) by teenagers as part of a high school course in caring for children in their schools (maybe, incidentally, making the day care workers into better parents in later life). The point is not for this report to come out with a proposal on how to provide low-cost high quality care. Rather, it is to suggest that licensing, with its rigidities, ensures that day care costs will continue to rise in the years to come.

What is necessary to protect parents is the complete openness of all day care centres to parental overview. Centres of whatever kind must be prepared to operate, as it were, in a fishbowl.[6] Day care centres should be embedded in the community, subject to both voice and exit, to both social and market control.

To assist parents in forming opinions before they make a choice, centres can be required to file with a licensing authority data on their organization and programs (data which would be checked by the authority). These data might include the number of adults working in the centre, when they work, their qualifications and salaries, the number of children in the centre, the physical characteristics of the centre, a breakdown on all costs, and finally the salary (and profits, if any) accruing to the centre operator. Parents would then have some idea of what they were paying for. The authority would verify these facts as well as check to ensure the child's safety. The authority might also solicit letters of opinion (to be kept on file) from randomly selected families that had used each centre.

If for-profit centres wish to operate in such an environment, they should be encouraged to do so. Of course, these are not the secretive *private* firms of traditional theory, but then the closed firm is not suited to this sector. Nor would all the requirements necessarily be more onerous than the current licensing requirements. For example, Miniskools already keeps a file of letters solicited from parents whose children are withdrawn from the centres for, like any profit maximizing firm, Miniskools seeks to maintain its clientele, and find out why parents exercising exit might be dissatisfied. When asked by this author how they might feel about a requirement to open their letter file to the public, the management was not at all hostile to the suggestion.

If some of the regulatory function of the Day Nurseries Branch disappears, its functioning to assist in raising standards should not. One possibility is to introduce certification. In regulation the public authority sets specific rules that must be observed in order to operate legally. In certification, by contrast, the government defines various classifications of day care. Any centre may operate, but only centres meeting the relevant criteria will be certified as such by the

6 This is an opinion the author has expressed elsewhere; see, for example, Nelson and Krashinsky (1974).

province. For example, the province might certify centres as either 'Minimum' or 'High' quality (To avoid a stigma of 'minimum' care, terms such as 'Standard,' 'Developmental,' 'Enriched,' and so on, could be used.) The public authority, using its considerable experience in day care, might also write up its own evaluation of each centre, the evaluation to be open to the public and subject to re-evaluation at any time at the discretion of the Branch or at the request of the centre, if it feels it has corrected past wrongs. The Day Nurseries Branch might also designate some centres as experimental to warn parents of the controversial nature of care in an unusual centre. Of course, for-profit firms in most sectors do not have to submit to these requirements, but day care is a very particular part of our economy. Parents may not agree with the judgments of the province. But those without strong opinions will have somewhere to start.

Finally, the Day Nurseries Branch should assist in the opening of co-operative centres and should offer its expertise to all ongoing centres. Since the co-operative form seems most suited to 'voice,' it should be encouraged by management advice, funds for initial capital investment, since capital funds are frequently a problem for all non-profit firms, and provision for bulk purchasing of food and equipment at discount prices. Ongoing supervision could be provided to all willing centres.

Day care seems optimally suited to both exit and voice. Any provincial system should allow for many types of day care to make exit more effective, and for requirements of openness to encourage voice.

CONCLUSION

A day care sector in which only for-profit firms operated would raise serious questions for those concerned about quality. The temptation would be present for any firm to try to raise profits by cutting quality in ways not easily perceived by the parent (assuming that day care is indeed a commodity that is difficult for parents to evaluate). But it would be false logic to conclude from that observation that no for-profit firms should be allowed to operate in the sector. Nor can one conclude that strict public regulation would provide the best quality of day care to children in Ontario.

The profit motive has much to commend it, particularly the responsiveness of firms, motivated by profits, to the needs of consumers. It appears that for-profit day care firms operate more in the public interest when they operate side by side within the sector with public and non-profit firms. The public firms set a standard for the type of care to be expected by parents, while non-profit firms aim at high quality private care. But neither mode is entirely responsive to consumers. A mix of centres would seem to serve parents and their children in the best way. This is especially true in an evolving sector, in which the desires of parents and the patterns of demand are still in flux.

Regulation is also seen as not being in the best interests of consumers. Regulation denies care to families that cannot afford the standard of care being regulated. And even for those who can afford regulated care, regulation tends to raise price by setting standards that in many cases are not directly related to quality. The key to day care quality is the devotion of the staff. Setting 'paper' qualifications inevitably will do little to ensure 'devotion' and 'love,' but will do much to raise costs by limiting those who can work in centres and by increasing training costs (which will be passed on to parents). Regulation assumes that the best way to provide day care is well-known and can be written down. In an evolving sector, this is counter-productive.

The basic problem is that parents have difficulty in evaluating care. This report suggests that the public interest is best served by attacking that problem directly. By requiring all centres to be open to parental overview, by having the public authority collect information to be made available to parents and certify centres, the province would have assisted parents in choosing a good centre. The goal is to protect the consumer without unduly restricting the ability of the market to respond to the needs of families.

7
Summary of findings and proposals for day care policy in Ontario

Between 1950-51 and 1966-67, expenditures by the Ontario Provincial Government on day care grew at a rate of about 5½ per cent per year, from just under $200,000 to just under $470,000. During the next eight years, expenditures grew at a rate of about 56 per cent per year, to over $16,000,000 in 1974-75. It is not clear that adequate consideration has been given to exactly what kind of day care program will finally result in Ontario, and to what the ultimate level of day care expenditures will be. It has been the purpose of this report to develop an economic analysis of day care policy so as to understand the impact of government actions and to assist in designing an optimal public policy for the future. Quite naturally, not all the issues can be resolved by economics. Much of the debate surrounding day care focuses on how income should be distributed. In particular, should the government assume a larger financial responsibility for children, or should the financial burden of children remain on the shoulders of their parents? Only when that question is answered can economic analysis indicate how best to structure day care policy in Ontario.

This final chapter is an attempt to summarize the findings of this report. For the summary, the report may be divided into three parts. Chapters 2 and 3 provided the background for the analysis of public policy. Chapters 4 and 5 investigated the rationales for day care subsidies and discussed how those subsidies should best be structured. Finally, Chapter 6 examined the provision of day care and the need for regulation.

(a) Background
Chapters 2 and 3 examined some of the facts underlying the growing use of day care in Ontario. The labour force participation rate for mothers has risen

dramatically in the decades since World War II, until in 1973 the labour force included two out of every five mothers and one out of every three mothers with preschoolers. Most of the children of these mothers are cared for through informal arrangements, that is, by babysitters and relatives, a significant number of whom are unpaid. Day care centres accounted for the care of only 7 per cent (one in fourteen) of the preschoolers aged three to five years with working mothers in 1973. This figure has been rising (it was only 3 per cent in 1967), reflecting, at least in part, the growing public subsidies to specific users of day care. In general, among parents who pay for their own day care, it would appear that unpaid arrangements (relatives, etc.) are the preferred form of care, irrespective of income.

All categories of day care centres have grown rapidly in Ontario in the last few years. These include municipal centres, private non-profit and private commercial centres, and co-operative centres. Public funding has played a major role, along with the growing number of children to be served. The big boom began in 1966 with the passing of the Canada Assistance Plan, which shared federally on a 50-50 basis the provinces' day care expenditures. As CAP was extended, Ontario encouraged municipalities to subsidize day care by paying 80 per cent of all costs (more during the Project Day Care in 1972, which combined winter works and the building of day care centres). Expansion is at present (1976) being choked off by limits on government expenditures.

The cost per child in a day care centre has also grown. In 1975, the yearly cost for one child aged four years in a day care centre was over $2400 in the municipal centres in Toronto, and about $1800 in the private centres in Toronto. The principal costs in day care centres are staff salaries. Since provincial law sets the minimum staff-child ratios, and since most centres, in fact, do not vary from these minimum requirements, the major variations in costs occur because of variations in salaries. Metro Toronto municipal centres lead the Province in salaries; private centres run somewhat behind. But even in the municipal centres, salaries are not high compared with other professions (public school teaching, for example).

There is some reason to fear that increasing public involvement and the increasing number of centres will further escalate costs. An examination of the private centres in Toronto currently selling day care to the municipality shows a tendency for costs to drift upward as the proportion of subsidized children in the centre grows. One explanation of this is that it is easier to induce governments to pay for higher costs than to get consumers to do the same. As the day care sector grows and public subsidy grows, one would expect workers in the centres to become more militant in their demands. And salaries will rise, if only because a growth in the sector will require the hiring of more workers who do not now wish to enter day care.

Quite naturally, high costs have led to attempts at cost reduction. But since quality is linked strongly to staff-child ratios, costs can be cut only if quality is reduced or if staff salaries fall. Quality reduction is dangerous; standards established nine years ago in the US would rate most Ontario centres barely above 'minimum.' Salary reductions are hard to achieve. One attempt to cut salaries is the introduction of private home day care, in which care is given by individuals in their own homes. But lower staff-child ratios necessary in homes make the author sceptical that *supervised* home care will significantly reduce costs.

(b) *Public policy regarding subsidies to day care*
Chapters 4 and 5 examined arguments for the government subsidizing the use of day care. It was shown that if the only goal of policy is to help families (or, for that matter, working women), then only limited subsidies to day care can be justified. In general, a reduction in the tax rate on the mother's earnings would be more efficient than an increase in the subsidy paid towards day care. This conclusion is derived from a mathematical model presented in the Appendix to Chapter 4. This model shows that the maximum subsidy to day care that can be justified by a desire to raise family utility is to allow day care payments to be tax deductible from income.

The same conclusion is reached by realizing that the day care subsidy acts for most families like an increase in the wage rate. The subsidy increases the net gain in the family's income when the mother works since the family pays less for day care, which is exactly what a wage subsidy would do. But a reduction in the tax rate on the parent's earnings (or a wage subsidy) is more efficient than subsidies for the purchase of day care.

Poor families are now offered subsidized day care irrespective of whether work by the mothers in the marketplace makes economic sense. Thus a family could conceivably receive over $9000 worth of day care (or more) to free a mother to work at the minimum wage. In addition, since current policy subsidizes only child care in formal centres, it provides a perverse incentive for poor families with perfectly acceptable low-cost high-quality arrangements available for their children – say a nearby trusted friend or relative – to use an expensive formal day care centre. But a reduction in the tax rate suffers none of these drawbacks. The family will still have the proper incentive to keep child care costs low, and the mother will have no economic incentive to work when the cost of child care exceeds the economic benefits of entering the labour force.

This result is independent of the decision on how much redistribution ought to take place towards families with children. In the extreme, if it was decided that the government were financially responsible for the care of all children, it would not be efficient to provide universal free day care. Rather, it would be most efficient to pay parents a large stipend towards the support of each child, and make any expenditures by the family on day care tax deductible.

Higher subsidies to day care can only be justified by a desire to improve the welfare of the children themselves rather than that of the whole family. In this case the report argues that the subsidy should reach all relevant children, not only the smaller group whose mothers work, or the even smaller group whose mothers work and use formal day care. A voucher plan is proposed. The voucher, issued to parents of all children in the target group, could be used for an enriched nursery school program (including transportation to and from the school) when the parent did not work. When the parent did work, the voucher could be used in a day care centre to defray part of the fee (paying for a specially enriched portion of the program). When the parent used other child care arrangements, the voucher would be used for nursery school. Since it would reduce the amount of time a babysitter would be required, there should be little problem in encouraging use of the voucher. Or it could be used even for an enriched program at the home of the sitter, if a number of children were involved and it was financially feasible.

Of course, the size of the voucher, the number of children covered by the program, and whether different sized vouchers would be given to particularly poor children are all political questions. But the principle of the voucher plan is not to limit whatever support is given to needy children to only those parents who work and use day care. The voucher scheme thus avoids the incentive problems of parents working and using day care only because it qualifies their children for subsidy.

The costs of any subsidization scheme would, of course, depend upon the level of subsidy. In general, the costs would be well above current costs in the province, because of the limited numbers of children now being served. A subsidy scheme such as that outlined above, aimed at all children aged two to four years, would cost in the order of $370,000,000.

Finally, the effect on fertility of the subsidization of day care is ambiguous. It is expected that an increase in day care subsidies would tend to increase labour force participation, because those subsidies act as a wage subsidy. It is not possible to develop firm projections of the size of such an increase. Using one set of estimates for labour supply elasticities, it can be estimated that a voucher scheme as outlined above might bring about 15,000 mothers into the labour force in Ontario.

(c) *Public policies regarding the provision of day care*
Chapter 6 examined arguments for government regulation of firms in the industry. Regulation of day care centres is based primarily upon the assumptions

that parents cannot judge the quality of day care sufficiently well to protect their children. Although the individuals in Ontario regulating the day care centres have been dedicated, and although regulation has served to upgrade standards in many centres, the chapter generally rejects regulation as an effective measure. First, since most of the child care sector is unorganized and unregulated, regulation cannot affect the majority of care arrangements. By maintaining minimum standards in day care centres, regulation denies to parents the option of purchasing lower-cost, below-standard day care, even if that care would be much more desirable than the current babysitting arrangements being made by the parent. Requiring high standards without ensuring that all families can afford the resulting high-cost care must be ineffectual.

Second, even if the first problem were removed, regulation is left with the problem of how to identify the characteristics of quality that one would like to regulate. If parents find judging day care difficult, it would seem even harder to write a set of legal regulations that can guarantee quality day care. Staff-child ratios are important and are regulated, but equally important is the quality of the people working in the centre. One danger with regulation is its frequent insistence on 'paper' (academic) qualifications. In fact, what is wanted in a centre is workers who are loving and competent – qualities hard to ensure by academic experience. And, of course, paper qualifications raise salaries and costs and drive day care out of the reach of many more families.

Yet regulation has helped to eliminate the most obvious abuses, and the educational function of the regulatory body would make its disappearance regrettable. Chapter 6 recommends an alternative, certification, in which different quality levels are defined by the province and centres are classified by quality. The province would also require centres to operate in a 'fishbowl,' open to constant parental overview. The certifying agency would encourage parents using a centre to write letters of evaluation, and then make these evaluations open to all parents interested in the particular centre. The province would also assist in the establishment of centres and the training of staff, continuing the tradition of participation in the upgrading of day care.

If the profit motive invites certain abuses, one alternative is, of course, to allow only non-profit and public centres into the sector. This idea is rejected. The search for profits may encourage low quality (in ways invisible to parents), but it also leads to very desirable characteristics: cost cutting (efficiency), responsiveness to the needs and desires of parents, willingness to expand to fill demand, etc. So long as for-profit firms are prepared to operate in an open environment, they should be welcomed to the sector. And, of course, public and non-profit firms provide examples to parents and other interested parties of the kind of quality possible at a given price. If for-profit centres cut quality too much, they must suffer by the comparison. This mix of centres allows good features of each mode of production to be manifested in the sector.

(d) Conclusion

It is difficult to separate out issues concerning the distribution of income from issues of how to design the most efficient public programs. In day care, it is natural for those interested in transferring income to working women to pick, for their fight, ground that is most attractive to the public. Good care for small children qualifies quite well. Changes in regulatory standards are fought, not because of the great virtues of regulation, but because of the changes in the level of subsidy if regulatory standards are eroded.

It may well be true that these issues will be decided with little concern for the efficiency arguments raised in this report. To this the economist can make two comments. First, it would be regrettable if income redistribution could only take place by introducing into the economy far more inefficiency than is 'required,' that is, the redistribution of income will be far more costly if undertaken through day care subsidies than if undertaken through other instruments, such as lowered tax rates and cash transfers, discussed earlier. Second, it would be regrettable if income redistribution were rejected only because day care subsidies are inefficient. Since far more efficient instruments exist to redistribute income, it would be false logic to determine the issue of redistribution by considering only subsidies to day care.

Bibliography

Abt Associates, Inc. (1971) *A Study in Child Care 1970-71* (OEO Contract Number OEO-B00-5213), 55 Wheeler Street, Cambridge, Massachusetts 02138, April

Akerlof, G.A. (1970) 'The market for "lemons": qualitative uncertainty and the market mechanism.' *Quarterly Journal of Economics* 84, 488-500

Arrow, K.J. (1963) 'Uncertainty and medical care.' *American Economic Review* 53, 947-968

Baumol, W.J. (1967) 'Macroeconomics of unbalanced growth: the anatomy of urban crisis.' *American Economic Review* 57, 415-26

Becker, G. (1965) 'A theory of the allocation of time.' *The Economic Journal* 75, 493-517

Becker, G.S. and H.G. Lewis (1973) 'On the interaction between the quantity and quality of children.' *Journal of Political Economy* 81, S279-S288

Birch, Margaret (1974) 'Statement to the legislature by the Honourable Margaret Birch provincial secretary for social development announcing day care services for children, June 4.' Xerox of speech

British Columbia (1975) 'Social Assistance Act,' B.C. Regulation 259/75, Order in Council 1138, effective 1 June, pamphlet

Cain, Glen G. and Harold W. Watts (1973) 'Towards a summary and synthesis of the evidence,' in G.G. Cain and H.W. Watts, *Income Maintenance and Labour Supply*, Institute for Research on Poverty Monograph Series (Chicago: Rand McNally)

Canada Assistance Plan, Department of Health and Welfare, *Canadian Day Care Survey (1972), Status of Day Care in Canada (1973)*, and *Status of Day Care in Canada (1974)*, all pamphlets available from National Day Care Information Centre, Canada Assistance Plan, Department of National Health and Welfare, General Purpose Building, Tunney's Pasture, Ottawa, Ontario K1A 1B5

The Canadian Council on Social Development (1972) *Day Care Report of a Naitonal Study by The Canadian Council on Social Development*, 55 Parkdale Avenue, Ottawa, Ontario, K1Y 1E5, January

Cicirelli, V.G. et al. (1969) 'The impact of Head Start; an evaluation of the effects of Head Start on children's cognitive and affective development.' Report of a study undertaken by Westinghouse Learning Corporation and Ohio University under contract B89-4536 dated 20 June 1968 with the Office of Economic Opportunity (Washington: Office of Economic Opportunity)

Cicirelli, V.G., J.W. Evans, and J.S. Schiller (1970) 'The impact of Head Start: a Reply to the Report Analysis.' *Harvard Educational Review* 40, 105-29

Clifford, Howard (1971) 'Debunking the day care mythology.' *Canadian Welfare* 47, 13-15, 30

Commissioner of Social Services, The Municipality of Metropolitan Toronto, Department of Social Services (1975) 'Projected five year program with respect to day care services.' Xerox, 12 May

Crozier, James (1975) Memo to Social Services Committee, re day care program-fee for service. 3 November

Diamond, P.A. and J.A. Mirrlees (1971) 'Optimal taxation and public production.' *American Economic Review* 61, 8-27, 261-78

Ditmore, J. and W.R. Prosser (1973) 'A study of day care's effect on labour force participation of low-income mothers.' Report to the Office of Economic Opportunity, Office of Planning, Research, and Evaluation, 1200 19th Street N.W., Washington, D.C. 20506, June (Report is available through the National Technical Information Service, U.S. Department of Commerce, Springfield, VA. 22151)

Downs, A. (1970) 'Competition and community schools.' In A. Downs, *Urban Problems and Prospects*. (Chicago: Markham Press)

Ekrem, R. (1973) 'Child care in Norway.' In Roby, *Child Care – Who Cares?*

Emlen, A.C. and J.B. Perry, Jr. (1974) 'Child care arrangements.' In L.W. Hoffman and F.I. Nye, *Working Mothers*. (San Francisco: Jossey Bass, Inc.)

Eskula, I. (1973) 'Children's day care in Finland.' In Roby, *Child Care – Who Cares?*

Family Day Care Services (1974) 'Some service statistics from Family Day Care Services.' Mimeo, provided by mail from the agency, 380 Sherbourne Street, Toronto, Canada

Ferge, S. (1973) 'The development of the protection of mothers and children in Hungary after 1945.' In Roby, *Child Care – Who Cares?*

Goldfarb, R.S. (1970) 'Comment' (on Hochman and Rogers, 1969). *American Economic Review* 60, 994-6

Heckman, J.J. (1974) 'Effects of child-care programs on women's work effort.' *Journal of Political Economy* 82, S136-S163

Hepworth, H. Philip (1975) *Personal Social Services in Canada: A Review, Vol 2, Day Care Services for Children.* The Canadian Council on Social Development, March

Hirschman, Albert O. (1970) *Exit, Voice, and Loyalty: Responses to Decline in Firms, Organizations, and States* (Cambridge: Harvard University Press)

Hochman, H.M. and J.D. Rogers (1969) 'Pareto optimal redistribution,' *American Economic Review* 59, 542-57

Hoffman, L.W. and F.I. Nye (1974) *Working Mothers.* (San Francisco: Jossey Bass, Bass, Inc.)

Karne, M. et al. (1973) 'Social rights in Sweden before school starts.' In Roby, *Child Care – Who Cares?*

Krashinsky, M. (1973) *Day care and public policy.* Unpublished PhD thesis, Yale University

Lalonde, M. (1973) Minister of National Health and Welfare, Government of Canada, Working Paper on Social Security in Canada, April 18

Lancaster, K.J. (1966) 'A new approach to consumer theory.' *Journal of Political Economy* 74, 132-57

– (1966) 'Change and innovation in the technology of consumption.' *American Economic Review* 55, 14-23

Leibowitz, A. (1974) 'Home investments in children.' *Journal of Political Economy* 82, S111-S131

Light, R.J. and P.V. Smith (1970) 'Choosing a future: strategies for designing and evaluating new programs.' *Harvard Educational Review* 40, 1-28

MacAvoy, P.W. (1970) *The Crisis of the Regulatory Commissions.* New York: W.W. Norton

Metropolitan Toronto, Department of Social Services (1975) 'Statistics for Robarts Commission, Nurseries and Day Care Centres.' Unpublished, xerox, provided by the Department of Social Services

Michael, R.T. (1973) 'Education and the derived demand for children.' *Journal of Political Economy* 81, S128-S164

Mishan, E.J. (1972) 'The futility of Pareto-efficient distributions.' *American Economic Review* 62, 971-6

Musgrave, R. (1970) 'Comment' (on Hochman and Rogers, 1969). *American Economic Review* 60, 991-3

Nelson, R.R. and M. Krashinsky (1974) 'Public control and economic organization of day care for young children.' *Public Policy*, 22, 53-75

Newhouse, J.P. (1970) 'Towards a theory of nonprofit institutions: an Economic model of a hospital.' *American Economic Review*, 60, 64-74

Nickson, May (1975) 'Preliminary report on working mothers and their child care arrangements in 1973,' Statistics Canada, Labour Division, Manpower Research and Development section. Xerox

Okun, A.M. (1975) *Equality and Efficiency, The Big Tradeoff* (Washington: Brookings Institution)

Ontario Economic Council (1976) *Issues and Alternatives, 1976, Social Security*. Pamphlet, Ontario Economic Council, 81 Wellesley Street East, Toronto, Ontario

Policy Secretariat, Ministry of Community and Social Services (n.d.) 'Towards a method for regional allocation of day nursery spaces.' Xerox, no date, but tables in the report are dated 1974

Province of British Columbia (1974) 'Services for people: annual report of the Department of Human Resources.' Pamphlet

Revenue Canada (1975) 'Your 1975 tax guide.' Pamphlet with the standard income tax forms

– (1975) Schedule 5, 'Child care expenses.' Income Tax Forms

Robertson, G. and P. Ferlejowski (1975) 'A comparative review of innovative working time arrangements in Ontario.' Employment Information Series, Research Branch, Ontario Ministry of Labour, October

Roby, P. (1973) *Child Care – Who Cares?*. (New York: Basic Books, Inc.)

Rowe, Mary P. (1971) 'The economics of child care.' *Hearings before the Committee on Finance, United States Senate, Ninety-second Congress, First Session on S.2003, Child Care Provisions of H.R.1 and Title VI of Printed Amendment 318 of H.R.1, September 22, 23, 24, 1975,* (Washington: U.S. Government Printing Office, pp. 235-313)

Sinclair, Michael (1975) 'Relationships between female labour force participation and day care services in Ontario: context, interactions, and public policy issues.' Unpublished xerox, August

Smith, M.S. and J.S. Bissell (1970) 'Report analysis: the impact of Head Start.' *Harvard Educational Review* 40, 51-104

The Social Planning and Research Council of Hamilton and District (1974) 'Day care needs of children in Hamilton and district (abridged version) July 1971.' Pamphlet, second printing, 153½ King Street East, Hamilton, Ontario L8N 1B1

Spence, M. (1972) 'Market signalling: the informational structure of job markets and related phenomena.' Harvard University, Kennedy School of Government, Public Policy Program, Discussion Paper Number 4.

Statistics Canada (1975) *The Labour Force*, September

Statistics Canada, Labour Force Survey Division (1975) 'Working mothers and their child care arrangements in Canada 1973.' *The Labour Force*, September, p. 84

Steinfels, M.O. (1973) *Who's Minding the Children? The History and Politics of Day Care in America* (New York: Simon and Schuster)

Takahashi, N. (1973) 'Child care programs in Japan.' In Roby, *Child Care – Who Cares?*

Trebilcock, M.J. (1976) 'Winners and losers in the modern regulatory state.' In K.J. Rae and J.T. McLeod, *Business and Government in Canada*, 2nd ed. (Toronto: Methuen Publications)

U.S. Department of Health, Education, and Welfare, Office of Child Development (1967) *Standards and Costs for Day Care.* Unpublished, xerox

Westinghouse Learning Corporation (Westat Research) (1971) *Day Care Survey 1970* (OEO Contract Number 800-5160), 16 April

Willis, R.J. (1973) 'A new approach to the economic theory of fertility behaviour.' *Journal of Political Economy* 81, S70-S95

Women's Bureau, Canada Department of Labour (1970) *Working Mothers and their Child-care Arrangements* (Ottawa: Queen's Printer)

Women's Bureau, Labour Canada (1975) *Women in the Labour Force, Facts and Figures* (Ottawa: Information Canada)

– (1975) 'Women and men in the labour force 1964 and 1974: annual averages calculated from monthly labour force survey of statistics Canada.' Xerox, 7 July

Young, D.R. and R.R. Nelson (1974) *Public Policy for Day Care of Young Children.* (Lexington, Mass.: Lexington Books)

Ontario Economic Council Research Studies

Ontario Economic Council Research Stu

11 Day Care and Public Policy in Ontario

M. KRASHINSKY

The last decade has seen rapid growth both in the use of extra-family care by wo
parents and in public involvement in the day care sector. This study, written fror
economic perspective, is an important contribution to the debate on public polic
tracing the development of day care in Ontario, the study focuses on two crucial
issues: should day care be subsidized and should the day care industry be regulat

Using a.sophisticated economic model, Professor Krashinsky demonstrates tha
Ontario subsidies to day care are an inefficient way to assist working parents. Ins
proposes a system of tax reductions which would enable many more families to t
vantage of a greater range of child care facilities. If subsidies are to help children,
argues, they must apply to all children in need, whether or not their parents worl
use day care. A general nursery school voucher system, he suggests, would be an
approach.

Although regulation in Ontario has been useful, Krashinsky suggests that the ¡
would be better served by an active public agency that restricted itself to collecti
disseminating information. He concludes that the province has been well served t
ture of public, private, and non-profit day care institutions and that each mode h
to play in an evolving sector.

This study will be of interest to both academics and practical policy-makers.

M. KRASHINSKY is a member of the Department of Economics at Scarborough C
University of Toronto.

ISBN 0-8020-3349-0

University of Toronto Press